A
Panorama of the
World's Legal Systems

A PANORAMA

of the

WORLD'S LEGAL SYSTEMS

by

JOHN HENRY WIGMORE

Professor of Law in Northwestern University

IN THREE VOLUMES
WITH FIVE HUNDRED ILLUSTRATIONS

VOLUME III

SAINT PAUL
WEST PUBLISHING COMPANY

A Panorama
of the World's Legal Systems

CONTENTS

———

VOLUME ONE

[IX]

VOLUME TWO

CHAPTER VIII.
THE JAPANESE LEGAL SYSTEM

CHAPTER IX.
THE MOHAMMEDAN LEGAL SYSTEM

CHAPTER X.
THE KELTIC LEGAL SYSTEM

CHAPTER XI.
THE SLAVIC LEGAL SYSTEM

CHAPTER XII.
THE GERMANIC LEGAL SYSTEM

VOLUME THREE

CHAPTER XV.

THE ROMANESQUE LEGAL SYSTEM

(I)   Resurrection of Justinian's Law-Books

(II)   Adaptation of Roman Law

[XII]

CHAPTER XVI.

THE ANGLICAN LEGAL SYSTEM

(I)   Building a Common Law

CHAPTER XVII.

EPILOGUE: THE EVOLUTION OF LEGAL SYSTEMS

APPENDIX

THE
MARITIME
LEGAL SYSTEM

Prologue to Chapters XIII, XIV, XV

The Germanic peoples had overspread all Europe west of Russia. Their political and legal system had now come to dominate, displacing or absorbing or penetrating, in variant degree, the original institutions of the Keltic and Slavic and Romanic areas thus occupied. But it developed at a slow pace, and it was unequipped in several elements to meet the new needs of the times. At this juncture, about the 1400's, it found flourishing alongside of it three other systems, which possessed its missing elements and competed to supply them.

These were the Maritime system of sea-law, the Papal system of church-law, and the resurrected legal science of Justinian. The grand phenomenon of the centuries A. D. 1100-1800 is the parallel growth and ultimate amalgamation of these four systems.

The three other systems had been growing up gradually, independent of any one race or people in their origin; but by this time the course of events was bringing them into close contact with the now widely spread Germanic institutions. All three were before long to be

[*871*]

absorbed and to lose their identity in the process of nationalization of law, now going on. But all three had their origins long before the 1400's. So it is now necessary to turn back for some centuries and to sketch their origin and progress.

And, first, the Maritime legal system.

XIII

The Maritime Legal System

(I) The Common Law of the Sea

1. Egyptians and Phoenicians.
2. Rhodian law.
3. Code of Amalfi.
4. Venice and Genoa.
5. Barcelona—Consulado del Mar.
6. Laws of Oleron—Oak Book of Southampton.
7. Sea-laws of Wisby—Hansa Shipping Ordinance—Shift of the centre of code-making from east to west and north.
8. Unity of evolution—Rules for jettison, compared.
9. Mariners' self-government.
10. Court-judgments—Legislative process in the Hansa ordinances.

(II) The National Laws of the Sea

11. French Marine Ordinance—Other national codes.

(III) The Common Law of the Sea, Once More

12. York-Antwerp Rules—Hague Rules of 1921.
13. The Bill of Lading as an international Common Law of the Sea.

XIII
The Maritime Legal System

THE earliest picture of a boat, found on an Egyptian vase, has been dated at some 6000 years B. C. The earliest recorded overseas expedition—that is, away from the coast—is that of an Egyptian king, dating about B. C. 2900. But the oldest picture of a sea-going ship of large size is the sculptured ship of Queen Hatsheput, in Egypt, about B. C. 1500.[1] This queen was already known to be a ruler of distinction; but owing to an inscription on Mt. Sinai, only deciphered

XIII. 1—QUEEN HATSHEPUT'S SHIP, B. C. 1500, IN EGYPT

[*875*]

in 1925, perhaps her greatest fame in future will be that she was the princess who discovered the infant Moses in the bulrushes and saved him to become the Hebrew leader.

The Egyptian maritime achievements were later overshadowed by the Phoenicians, who made themselves masters of the Mediterranean for many centuries. Then came the Greeks, their rivals and successors as maritime traders. And so the names of Phoenicia, with its great coast cities, Tyre and Sidon, and of Rhodes, the island at the eastern end of the Grecian Archipelago, are inseparably associated with the beginnings of maritime law.

(I) THE COMMON LAW OF THE SEA

1. The sea-traffic must have been enormous. Tyre, a Phoenician city, had probably more than a million population; Carthage, another Phoenician city, seven hundred thousand; Alexandria, a Greek city, the world's grain market, had one million. In the period five centuries before Christ, the coasts of the Mediterranean, as the map shows,[2] were already dotted with colonies and trading-posts, from end to end. And when it is remembered that for 3000 years before Christ the several nations swarmed with their ships trafficking along all the shores of this inland ocean, one can realize how the sea-commerce of the Mediterranean has formed a continuous body of custom dating back at least 5000 years before today. The empires

[*876*]

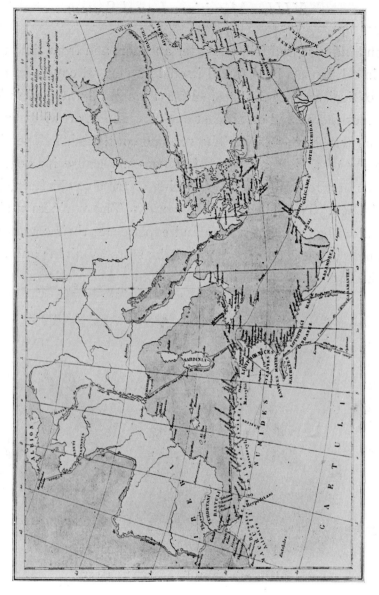

XIII. 2—COLONIES OF THE MEDITERRANEAN, B. C. 500

[877]

on land rose and fell, one after another; and from time to time Europe's land found itself in a general condition of political and legal chaos. But through all these vicissitudes there lived on at least one continuous, growing, and mature body of law. The sea law continued, independently of racial and dynastic changes, because its vogue was in a region owned by no king or tribe or chieftain,— the Sea. The galleys were its home.[3] The mariners of all waters had a common life and experience; their common guide was the sun by day and the stars by night; and so the common custom of sea-merchants was sea-law.

XIII. 3—A Greek Five-Banked Galley

1. Earliest Maritime Peoples

This formed a system by itself. Centuries later, it was destined to be absorbed into the various territorial national laws. But for nearly five thousand years it lived its own separate existence,—formulated by no sovereign, yet gradually codified, and obeyed by all. How separate it was, in its supremacy, can be realized from an anecdote in the Roman Digest, preserved in Greek;[4] it reads: "A certain man brought a case about shipwreck to the

XIII. 4—ROMAN DIGEST: THE LEX RHODIA

Emperor Antoninus, for decision; but the Emperor replied: 'I am indeed the supreme lord of the land. But Custom is the lord of the sea. Let this case be decided by the sea-law of the Rhodians, which our law accepts'."

This body of sea-law, in pre-historic times, had begun with the Phoenicians. But its leadership gradually shifted west and north with the expansion of commerce.

[*879*]

The history of this shifting is the history of maritime law.

2.   No record of Phoenician sea-law has survived. But tradition has perserved a few of the sea-rules of Rhodes, which became the next leading centre to be heard of.   Rhodes was one of the large Greek islands lying eastward towards Egypt.   Rhodes reached the height of its prosperity about B. C. 300.   It had succeeded to the primacy of Athens as the emporium of Greek commerce and a centre of arts and letters.   The massive bronze Colossus,[5] one hundred and five feet high, which was located on the pier at the entrance to its harbor, was deemed one of the seven wonders of the ancient world; when its fallen remnants were sold for metal, A. D. 600, it took nine hundred camels to carry them off.   Young men were sent to Rhodes from other cities to learn commercial methods; and the world-famous statue of the Laocoön was made by a Rhodian artist.   The city was said to contain three thousand marble statues.   The port of Rhodes had six practicable harbors; and the Rhodians were termed "the masters of the sea".   No authentic text of the Rhodian Code has survived.   But all sea-law for the ensuing thousand years was known as the Rhodian law.

3.   Then, as commerce shifted, the next code of general vogue was that of Amalfi, not far from Naples;[6] for the centre was again shifting west.   The Code of

XIII. 5—The Colossus at Rhodes

3. *Code of Amalfi*

XIII. 6—AMALFI, FROM THE SEA

Amalfi was formulated in the 1000's. Amalfi is now a small town of five thousand souls; and nothing is left but its Cathedral to testify to the prosperity and fame which enabled its sea-law to command respect 900 years ago. But in its brief day it was immensely rich, with a population of fifty thousand, and colonies in Syria, Arabia, India, and Africa. The Amalfitans claimed and were long reputed to have invented the mariner's compass; the crest of the city bore the motto: "Prima dedit nautis usus magnetis Amalphis". Even as late as A. D. 1570, a mercantile author, Freccia, declared that Amalfi's Code eclipsed the Rhodian law, for "all disputes, all lawsuits,

[*881*]

and all sea-controversies were decided by the law of Amalfi.''

The text of the Code of Amalfi was lost for centuries, and was only re-discovered in 1843, in an obscure manu-script in Vienna, carried off from Venice by the Austrians; its common name, as the title shows, was the Tablet of Amalfi;[7] for it was perhaps inscribed on tablets nailed up in public.

4. Each one of these commercial coast-towns had its own book of sea-law,—Venice, Pisa, Genoa, and a hundred others. But none of these three greatest commercial cities of the Italian Middle Ages seems to have impressed its leadership on the maritime common law.

Venice became famous for its government, and par-ticularly its Council of Ten. In a record of one of the

CAPITULA ET ORDINATIONES CURIAE MARITIMAE

NOBILIS CIVITATIS AMALPHAE

quae in vulgari sermone dicuntur:

LA TABULA   AMALFA

XIII. 7—THE CODE OF AMALFI

[*882*]

XIII. 9—GATE OF PLACARDS, VENICE
Here were posted the Judgments of the Council

judgments of the Council of Ten in a criminal case, dated September 10, 1708,[8] the sentence reads that three of the culprits be "cut so that their head is separated from their body and they die", and that the other three "be hung by the neck so that they die". These judgments were printed as leaf-

BANDO,
ET SENTENZA
DELL' ECCELSO
Conseglio di Dieci.

CONTRO

Il Dottor Giuseppe ⎫
Prè Francesco, e ⎬ Fratelli Gratioli Figlioli di
Girolamo ⎭ Pietro Alberto.
Francesco Badinelli.
Vicenzo, e ⎫ Figlioli di esso Francesco
Cosmo Badinelli ⎭ detti Battari.

Stampato per Pietro Pinelli,
Stampator Ducale.

XIII. 8—A JUDGMENT
OF THE VENETIAN COUNCIL OF TEN

lets, a copy was posted at the entrance to the Ducal Palace, called the Gate of Placards,[9] and other copies sent to all the local magistrates. The Council of Ten held its meetings in a room in the Ducal Palace, magnificently decorated with frescoes by some of Venice's greatest painters,—an example which should be imitated in our own courts of justice. The adjacent room was the chamber of the celebrated Inquisitors, who interrogated the accused before he was brought in to trial before the Council. And the square panel in the wall at the lower

[*883*]

left corner of the picture concealed the box in which anonymous complaints were dropped; for on the other side of the wall, in the public corridor, was a slit with a lion's head, called the Lion's Mouth (or "bussola"), into which papers might be inserted without revealing the informant's identity.[10]

Genoa was famous for its inventiveness in commercial methods. The Bank of St. George,[11] founded about A. D. 1400, and long the greatest of its kind, still stands, down at the city's water-front; and the archives of Genoa contain some of the earliest known examples of bills of

XIII. 10—Chamber of the Inquisitors, Venice

[*884*]

exchange and policies of marine insurance.

But neither Genoa nor Venice, even at the height of their sea-powers, ever set the standard for marine law.

5. We hear of no common code for another two or three centuries after the Amalfi Code, when the centre is now found shifting again westward to

XIII. 11—BANK OF ST. GEORGE, AT GENOA

Barcelona.[12] A papal official, describing Barcelona at the end of the 1400's, said of its laws: "In almost every maritime city the controversies of mariners and of merchants are settled by them, or by laws derived from them, with the greatest authority; and as formerly men spoke of the laws of Rhodes, now everyone speaks of the laws of Barcelona."

The Code of Barcelona was known as the Consulado del Mar, or Book of the Jurisdiction of the Sea, and first took shape in the 1200's; one of the best manuscripts is in

[*885*]

XIII. 12—BARCELONA, FROM THE SEA

the National Library at Paris.[13] The Consulado del Mar
was written originally in Catalan, the language of Barcelona. It was first printed in 1494; but the fourth edition
of 1523 is probably the only early edition now to be found
outside of a few European public libraries.[14]

The provisions of the Consulado were more diffuse and
its details more elaborate than in any other of these sea-
codes. It contained some two hundred and fifty short
chapters; and their style may be gathered from this passage, in Chapter 80, about the rights of the mariner to his
wages:[a]

[*The Consulado del Mar, chap. 80.*] "Further you should know
that the managing owner of a ship ought not to dismiss a mariner

XIII. 13—THE CONSULADO DEL MAR (MS.)
The title, in the middle of the left column, reads: "Dels bons stabli-
ments e costumes de la mar", and the text begins, "These are
the good rules and customs. . . which our ancestors made"

Segueire lo Libre de Consolat nouament
corregit: y stampat. Enlo qual son tengudes
les leys: e ordinacions dels actes maritims:
e Mercantiuols.   Et primo.

En qual manera son
elets los consols e lo jutge de les
appellacions quascun Any.
¶ Capitol primer.

Uascun any
lo vespre ôla festa de
Nadal ô nostre Sê
yor los promens na
uegants patrons ma
riners: ho partida de aquells a ple
guen consell enla eglesia de sancta
Tecla de's ciutat de Ualencia. E
aqui per eleccio: e no per redolins
tots en vna côcordants o la maior
partida elegeirê dos bons homês
dela art de mar en Côsols. ¶ E vn
home dela dita art dela mar: e no
de algûa a'tra art: ho hofficī: o sciê
cia en jutge deles appellacions: q̄s
fan deles sentencies dels dits con
sols. E les dites elecciôs son fetes
per priuilegi que los promens dela
dita art dela mar han del Senyor
r y: e de sos antecessors.

Del juramet que fan
los consols.   Capitol.ij.

O dia ô nadal los dits
consols elets juren en
poder dela justicia ci
uil ôla dita ciutat dis
la esglesia ô nostra do:
na sancta maria ôla seu: apres quel
dit justicia s jurat en poder del sen
yor Rey: ho de son batle: que be
e lealment se hauran enlo offici del
dit consolat: que daran diet axi al
maior: com el menor: e al menor cô
al maior: saluant tota hora la fael
tat: e lealtat del Senyor Rey.

Coz lo jutge dapells
es prelentat: e com jura.
Capitol.iij.

Pssada la dita festa de
nadal los côsols ab al
guns promens de mar
presenten lo dit jutge e
let al portât veus al p
curadôr enlo regne de Ualêcia: ho
a son lochtinent: e jura en poder da
quell: que be e lealment se haura en
lo dit offici. E aquell qui p los dits

a

XIII. 14—THE CONSULADO, IN CATALAN

from the ship until the voyage is concluded, except for three things, in the first place for robbery, in the second place for quarrelling, and in the third place if he does not obey the orders of the mate. The mate, however, ought not to command him to do anything which is not within his command, and the mariner ought not to be dismissed upon the first occasion of disobedience, but only upon the fifth occasion. . . . .

"Further, the managing owner of the ship is bound to the mariner, that if the mariner has agreed with the managing owner of the ship for a high rate of wages, and the managing owner of the ship shall find another mariner at a lower rate of wages, he cannot dismiss him from the ship so that he shall not sail in it, after he has once agreed and shaken hands upon it; for he is bound to observe such an agreement, as if it were entered in the ship's register.

"Further, the managing owner of the ship is bound to the mariner, that if the mariner has agreed with the managing owner of the ship, the latter cannot dismiss the mariner to make place for a relative or another man after his name has been entered in the ship's register, or after they have shaken hands, whether or not he has been received on board ship; and if he wishes to dismiss him he must pay him his wages precisely as if he had completed all his services during the voyage.

"Further, the managing owner is bound, if the mariner has worked for three days and is taken ill, to pay him half his wages, and if he cannot embark on the ship, he ought to dismiss him, if the mariner judges that he cannot go; and if he is in a strange place, the managing owner of the ship has to give him half his wages, whether or not he has money enough to pay them, and if he have not money enough, he must borrow it, for it is incumbent that the mariner should have his wages; and if the managing owner dies, his executors ought to discharge this obligation.

"Further, the managing owner is bound to the mariner, that if the mariner falls sick and dies in the vessel, he ought to be paid all his wages, and if he has on board any relative, the effects of the deceased should be given up to him, and, whether the deceased has said so or not, shall be handed over to his children or his wife, if they were living with him whilst he was alive. And if his wife was not loyal to him, or was not living with him when he was last on shore, or shall have run away after his departure, the managing owner of the ship with the ship's clerk, with the consent of the courts, shall give them to his nearest relatives.

"The mariner who shall be engaged for the voyage and shall die by the will of God before the ship has sailed, ought to have a quarter of his wages, which should be assigned and given to his heirs. Further, if he shall die after the vessel has set sail, and before she arrives at her port of destination, the half of his wages shall belong to the deceased, and shall be given to his heirs; and if he shall have received all his wages before he dies, the whole ought to belong to him and be given to his heirs, and the managing owner of the ship cannot dispute anything, nor claim anything back.

"If the mariner is engaged by the month and dies, his heirs should be paid for all the time which he has served.

"Further, the managing owner is bound to pay to the mariner his wages at the place where the merchandise pays freight."

The extensive vogue of the Consulado caused it to be translated into several languages, for the benefit of mariners of other countries. An edition was printed as far east as Venice, in 1566, in an Italian translation;[15] and indeed some Italian scholars once claimed Italy as the place of its origin. And other editions were printed as far north as Amsterdam, in Dutch and Italian, in 1704 and

LIBRO
DEL CONSOLATO
DE' MARINARI.

Nelquale fi comprendono tutti gli ſtatuti, & ordini
diſpoſti da gli antichi per ogni caſo di Mercantia,
ò di Nauigare, coſi à beneficio de' Marinari, come
de' Mercanti, & Patron de' Nauilij.

*Con l'aggiunta delle ordinationi ſopra l'Armate
di Mare, ſicurtà, entrate, & uſcite.*

DI NVOVO RISTAMPATO, ET
con ogni diligentia corretto.

IN VENETIA,
Per Andrea Rauenoldo.
M D LXVI.

XIII. 15—The Consolato, in Italian

XIII. 16—The Consolato, in Dutch

1723.[16] Its vogue thus extended through five centuries.

6. But in the meantime, new trade centres were starting in the north; and in the A. D. 1200's and 1300's a new codification had obtained vogue, named from the island of Oleron, off New Rochelle, in the Bay of Biscay,[17]— a region which was then English territory. There is a manuscript of it in the British Museum;[18] for this code was used by English and Scotch and Norman mariners also. Southampton was then one of England's great seaports; the Oak Book was the book of local customs of that seaport; and a fine MS. copy of the Laws of Oleron dating from about A. D. 1300 has recently been brought to light in the Oak Book of Southampton.[19] So closely was the Code of Oleron associated with English maritime customs that its authorship used to be attributed to King Richard the Lionhearted, when he returned from the Crusades.

7. The Laws of Oleron served as a sea-code for northwestern Europe for several centuries. But meantime, the Hansa League of the Baltic had come to dominate northern commerce all the way from Hamburg and Bremen to Novgorod in Russia. Its headquarters were first at Wisby on the island of Gotland, in the north Baltic, and hence its code was at first known as the Sea-Laws of Gotland. Wisby had some twelve thousand merchants in the 1200's; but it was destroyed and plundered by King

XIII. 17—THE ISLAND OF OLERON

[894]

XIII. 18—THE LAWS OF OLERON

XIII. 19—THE OAK BOOK OF SOUTHAMPTON
In this book was discovered in recent times a manuscript
text of the Laws of Oleron

XIII. 20—Wisby's Gate and Island
This town gave the name to a maritime code for northern commerce

Waldemar of Denmark in 1361, and never recovered from the blow.[20] The centre then shifted to the north German towns. In A. D. 1367 at the town hall in Cologne the delegates of seventy-seven cities met and formally organized the Hansa League.

The League became one of Europe's great powers. Its rules were more potent, in its field, than those of pope or emperor; for it could ruin a commercial town by its boycott. The Hansa had colonies everywhere in Europe. The most southerly site was at Venice, where today may still be seen the Fondaco dei Tedeschi, or Warehouse of the Germans. The most northerly centre was Bergen, on the coast of Norway;[21] and the long row of twenty-two buildings of the Hansa, which dominated the water-front, re-

XIII. 21—THE HANSA YARD AT BERGEN, NORWAY

XIII. 22—THE HANSA STEELYARD, LONDON

mains intact today. Some three thousand souls here formed the Hansa staff, all vowed to celibacy, and organized in guilds, each representing a foreign city. In London, the Hansa was equally strong; their establishment, known as the Steelyard[22] (because there stood the great city-scales for weighing all imports), was located just above London Bridge, at the only water-gate of the city, thus commanding the key to the whole foreign commerce of London. Bremen was one of the League's strongholds in Germany. But the most frequent meeting-place of the League Council was at Lübeck.[23] This city and Bremen were the last two members of the Hansa; for its power gradually declined, and in 1630 at Lübeck at its last general meeting only Lübeck and Bremen sent delegates.

The Hansa League had adopted the Sea-Laws of Wisby, which themselves were an adaptation of the earlier Laws of Oleron. An edition of the Hansa Code, printed at Lübeck in the year 1657, calls itself the Hansa Towns' Shipping Ordinance.[24]

Thus, the centre of fashion, in maritime code-making, had swung gradually around west and north,[25] through

XIII. 23—The Town Council House at Lübeck

[899]

Der Erbaren
Hansee-Städte
Schiffs = Ordnung
vnd See-Recht.
Deren sich ihre Bürger / sonderlich die Schiffs-
Rehdere / Befrachtere / Schiffer vnd Schiffs-
volck zu verhalten.

Von newem übersehen vnd gebessert / vnd vnter
gewisse Titul außgetheilet

Lübeck.
In verlegung Michel Volcken/
Gedruckt durch sel: Schmalhertzens Erben.
ANNO
M. DC. LVII.

XIII. 24—THE HANSA SHIPPING ORDINANCE

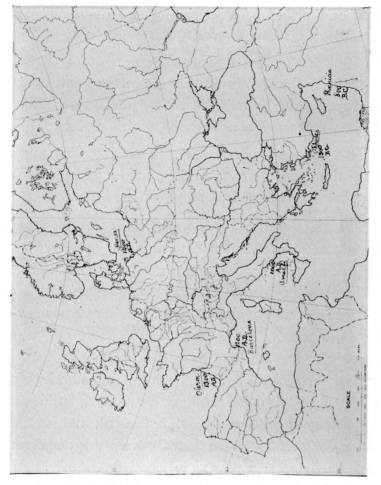

XIII. 25—Map of the Shift of Maritime Codes

three quarters of a circle, during two thousand years, from Rhodes, through Amalfi, Barcelona, Oleron, up to Wisby and Lübeck.

8. Now the remarkable feature in these several successive codes is the unity of their evolution as a single, distinct, and continuous body of maritime custom.

To illustrate this, let us take, almost at random, one of the distinctive features of sea-law, not found in land-law, —jettison—and trace it through all the codes.

The act of casting goods overboard in a storm to save the ship and its contents is known in sea-law as jettison; and when by jettison one man's goods are sacrificed, the others whose property is thus saved must repay him, each a ratable share. But there was, in the old common law of the sea, a peculiar provision for the procedure to be followed. In the Rhodian law as phrased in Greek at Byzantium, about A. D. 700, Article 9 says on this point: "If the captain is deliberating about jettison, let him ask the passengers who have goods on board, and let them take a vote what is to be done." Note this democratic idea of a joint enterprise; the merchants must first be consulted before the captain can lawfully jettison.

This feature has totally disappeared in modern law. But we can trace it for nearly 2000 years in the old law.

Going west in the line of evolution, we next find it persisting in Art. 48 of the Code of Amalfi. This draftsman, a philosopher, adds naively: "If the merchants are greedy, as some people always are, and would rather die on the spot than sacrifice anything, so that by their extreme avarice they refuse to jettison, then the captain after protest may proceed to jettison."

Then two centuries later, in the Consulado del Mar, of Barcelona, the same rule reappears, with much elaboration; here, the author provides a set speech which the captain must deliver in the presence of the mate and all on board: "Gentlemen, if we do not lighten the vessel we run great risk of losing our lives and everything; but if you, gentlemen, consent to lighten ship, then by God's will we can save ourselves and a large part of our goods; but if we do not cast them over, we shall lose ourselves as well as all that we have"; then if all or the majority of the merchants consent, the jettison may be made; but one of the merchants must first cast over something, then the captain may cast over the remainder.

Next, in the Laws of Oleron, the same rule is found once more, here again supplying the captain with a speech, but a shorter one than in the Consulado.

And finally in the Wisby Code and the Hansa Code, Title VII, Art. II, it appears once more, with little change, but without the words of the speech. And a notable thing, which marks the world-wide universality of sea-rules, is that in a sea-code of the Malay Islands, in the East Indies, dating back to the first Mohammedan Sultan, in the 1200's, is found an explicit provision of this identical nature, calling for a consultation of the merchants, and fixing the rule for counting the votes of each.

This provision about the formality of jettison serves to illustrate the continuity and identity of the common law of the sea through nearly two thousand years.

9. All of these sea-codes purported to represent the custom of the sea,—not the law of any territorial prince. They grew as the anonymous embodiment of these common customs. The title and opening sentence of the Consulado, as of most of the others, reads: "Aci commencen les bones costumes de la mar", "Here commence the good customs of the sea. These are the good establishments and the good customs on matters of the sea, which the wise men who traveled over the world commenced to give to our predecessors, who put them into books of the wisdom of the good customs". These codes owed their force to no prince or king or republic; and no jurist's name was associated with any of them as its original author or draftsman. Even the very city in which they originally took form was sometimes uncer-

tain; for Pisa and Marseilles, as well as Barcelona, once disputed for the place of origin of the Consulado del Mar.

And these customs, as rules, were enforced by special maritime courts elected by the guilds of the sea-trades, not by the ordinary territorial courts of the prince or seignior. Genoa, Pisa, Barcelona, and all the great mercantile sea-ports had each its court of the sea. This self-government of the sea by its own customs is illustrated in the opening sentence of a Spanish ordinance of A. D. 1283, sanctioning the Court of the Consuls at Valencia, and often prefixed to editions of the Consulado del Mar:[b]

[*The Sea-Guilds Elect Their Judges.*] "Every year, after noon on the day of Noel or Our Lord's Nativity, the elders of the sea-guilds, the masters, and the mariners, or any of them, meeting in council at the church of St. Pecla, in the city of Valencia, shall by vote (not by lot), whether unanimous or by majority, choose [two] good men of the sea-trade to be consuls, and one other man (of the same trade, not of any other trade or learning or position) to be judge of appeal from the judgments of the former; the said elections being held by privilege of the elders of the guild of the sea held of the king and his predecessors.

"After the said feast of Noel, the said consuls, with some elders of the sea, will present the said elected judge of appeal before the attorney-general of the Kingdom of Valencia or his deputy; there he will take oath to behave well and legally in his office; and he who is thus presented as judge of appeals before the attorney-general must be received by him in that post; for such has been the custom, notwithstanding that by the king's charter granted to the elders of the sea it is said that annually the judge shall be chosen 'by the king or his attorney-general', for neither the king nor his attorney-general has ever exercised this power, the above mentioned formalities being the only ones used.

"The consuls shall judge all questions of freight. . . . . . [etc., etc.], and generally all contracts mentioned in the Customs of the Sea. . . . . . The judgments given by the consuls and the judge shall read 'according to the Customs of the Sea', and shall conform to what is laid down in the several chapters of that book."

10.   These codes, no doubt, were usually in their origin the outgrowth of a long succession of decided causes; they summed up in convenient form the result of numerous judgments on important typical cases. Indeed, the Laws of Oleron were often entitled "the Judgments of the Sea", and each of their paragraphs is in form a ruling on a case put; thus:

"A ship departs from Bordeaux or elsewhere; it happens sometimes that it is lost, and they save the most they can of the wine and other goods. The merchants and the master are in great dispute, and the merchants claim from the master their goods. They may well have them, paying the freight for such part of the voyage as the ship has made, if it please the master. . . . . . *And this is the judgment in this case.*"

But this process of formation can no longer be traced. Probably no records were kept by these courts. Even of the English royal admiralty court no records are found before A. D. 1520. Of these earlier local courts of sea-law in the sea-towns no annals of their judgments appear to be extant, no collections of plea-rolls, no eye-witness reports of the trials.[c]

[*906*]

10. *Legislative Growth*

Some, however, of the codes exhibit a genuine legislative process. It was a favorite theory of Sir Henry Maine that the judicial process, in history, invariably preceded the legislative, i. e. that the period of code-formulation was preceded by a period of case-judgments. But in the history of the Hansa Towns' Shipping Code, at least, this theory is not verified. We there see a long succession of genuinely legislative enactments, covering three centuries, from a few brief measures of the 1300's, developing by A. D. 1614 into a complete topical code of fifteen chapters and one hundred and three sections, and proceeding constantly by way of legislative amendment, supplement and revision.

The Hansa Ordinance of A. D. 1482 is an interesting illustration of this process.[d] The Ordinance of A. D. 1470 already had some thirty sections. But in A. D. 1481 there was a strong demand to correct certain abuses in seafaring. In March, a meeting of the Hansa shipmasters, held at Bergen in Holland, drew up a list of their troubles; the misbehavior of the mariners (they averred) was making sea-traffic no longer possible; "everyone of these unruly fellows does just what he pleases, and makes so much mischief and trouble for the shipmasters that we shall have to give up sailing the seas unless you gentlemen can do something to alter this." Their list of grievances and proposed remedies read thus:

[*Complaint of the Hansa Shipmasters, December, 1480.*] "These are the complaints and grievances which the shipmasters of the Hansa delivered to the aldermen at Bruges about the mariners, and requested their despatch to the gentlemen of the towns indorsed hereon, so as to obtain remedy and correction thereof:

"I. First, the shipmasters request, from the authority of the gentlemen of the Hansa Towns, that whenever a shipmaster hires his crew for a round-trip voyage, the hire be given in three parts, to wit, the first part when the ship sails, the second part when the ship unloads at the port of destination, and the third when the ship wins home on the full voyage, and that the crew be holden and bound to help unload and ballast, so that it may lie in the stream without danger or risk.

"II. Item, a steersman engages himself to a shipmaster, and whenever it comes to pass that he is not good and competent for what he engaged for, so that the shipmaster's life and ship and the merchant's goods are endangered, it seems proper to the aforesaid shipmasters that to such a steersman should be given no more than half of a mariner's hire and subsistence, provided the shipmaster can make good proof with two good men or with his crew that the steersman was not good enough for what he engaged himself.

"III. Item, likewise, if a mariner engages himself to a shipmaster, and he is not good enough for what he engaged himself, then to such a mariner should be given no more than the half hire and subsistence, provided the shipmaster can prove it as above.

"IV. Item, whenever a steersman or mariner deserts the shipmaster, taking the wages that have been given him, the shipmasters request that such a steersman or mariner be flogged, wherever he may be found, or that he be branded with a boathook upon his cheek or elsewhere, so that he may be an example to others to avoid such conduct.

"V.   Item, it happens that a shipmaster has in his ship one or two of his crew who behave so rascally that the shipmaster must needs lay them off; the shipmasters request that such evil-doers should be given neither hire nor subsistence.

"VI.   Item, it happens also that there are some others who join with such evil-doers and lay off with them, to the discomfiture of the shipmaster; the shipmasters likewise request that to such be given neither hire nor subsistence, so as to be an example to others to avoid such conduct.

"VII.   Item, it is oft the case that a ship is loaded for a certain port, and that the crew makes mutiny on the sea and sails the ship without necessity or need into another port, against the will of the shipmaster; the aforesaid shipmasters request that to such men neither hire nor subsistence be given before the time when the ship is brought to the port whither loaded.

"VIII.   Item, the shipmasters request that the aforesaid gentlemen of the Towns will ordain what shall be given to the crew for their subsistence whenever the shipmaster comes from the east with a cargo of grain, and what the merchant shall give for primage; for the shipmasters and the merchants alike are on this subject much embarrassed by the crews' demands.

"IX.   Item, it happens that a shipmaster is loaded for a distant voyage, and the shipmaster from some event of necessity lays up the ship in dock before completing the voyage, and the merchants and the ship's friends decide that the shipmaster must continue the voyage, and the crew will not continue it; the shipmasters request that such persons be given neither hire nor subsistence before the time that the voyage is completed.

[*909*]

"X. Item, on these and many more like points, too long to be written, the aforesaid shipmasters request the aforesaid gentlemen of the Hansa Towns to provide remedies and amendments, and to uphold them with heavy penalties and fines, and also to correct and punish the offenders, so as to be an example to others to avoid such conduct."

This memorial was circulated by the Bruges authorities to Danzig, Lübeck, and other principal Hansa towns; and next year, at the Hansa Assembly of Sept. 16, 1481, at Lübeck, the record showed the following consideration given:

[*Hansa Proceedings of Sept. 18, 1481.*] "Afternoon at two of the clock assembled again at the Council House of Lübeck messieurs the aforesaid Councillors Plenipotentiary. . . . . . .

"Par. 36. Then was read a letter of the merchants of Bruges telling of the numerous misdoings of ship-crews, and a document enclosed therewith with proposals for remedying and punishing these misdoings.

"Par. 37. Item, was read a resolution, adopted by the Council of Lübeck, for the correction of the misdoings of steersmen and mariners, and for the punishment of the offenders; which in all its articles, after ample consideration of all articles, was approved, agreed, and adopted by messieurs the Councillors Plenipotentiary.

"Par. 38. Item, it was resolved to send the above-named articles to the Danzig Council, to receive their assent and approval."

After further interim correspondence, the ordinance came up for final action at the assembly of April 22, 1482, held at Lübeck; the record reads:

[*910*]

XIII. 26—The Hansa Fleet's Home-Coming at Lübeck

Lübeck was the most powerful city in the League, and its last stronghold. Even under the North German Confederation of the late 1800's, Lübeck retained a semi-independence

10. *Legislative Growth*

[*Hansa Proceedings of April 22, 1482.*] "In the year of our Lord 1482, at Lübeck,. . . on Monday at eight of the clock at the Council House in the presence of the honorable Council thereof were assembled [naming the delegates]:

"Par. 15. Item, was then read the ordinance and amendments made for the misdoings of mariners, and the revised articles forwarded from Danzig, of which a part was approved and a part altered".

And so, with the labors of the assembly ended, and the fur-robed merchant-princes ("ambassadors plenipotentiary" they proudly styled themselves) ready to start homeward in their ships of the Hansa fleet, riding at anchor in the harbor of Lübeck,[26] the ordinance was finally promulgated on May 4, 1482:

[*Hansa Ordinance of May 4, 1482.*] "In the interest of all seafarers and shippers, the honorable merchants of the six Wendish Towns, by their Councillors Plenipotentiary, meeting in assembly at Lübeck in this year 1482, in the name and on behalf of the united Hansa Towns, have proposed, approved, and enacted the following ordinance and articles, which they will cause strictly to be observed:

"I. Item, it is ordained that when a mariner shall be engaged in the Baltic sea or in Prussia, to make a full voyage either to England or to Flanders westward, or to Holland, Zeeland, Friesland or elsewhere, and even to the Gulf, he shall be paid his hire at three periods. When he engages himself, the first part of his hire shall be given him; and when they unload at the port of destination, the second part of the hire; and the third part of the hire shall be given him when the voyage is fulfilled. The mariners shall be bound, after voyage done, to bring the ship into the port and town whence it started, or wherever it pleases the shipmaster to bring it back

"II. Item, the like shall apply to sailors engaged at Lübeck to go to Livland and return to Lübeck or to go to Flanders or to Norway and return to Lübeck.

"III. Item, whoever is engaged for half a voyage, to him shall the half of his hire be given when he sails off and the other half when he arrives.

"IV. And every mariner, whoever he may be, shall be holden and bound to help load, unload, and ballast the ship on which he sails, so that it may lie in the stream without danger or risk, on penalty of forfeit of the hire due to him.

"V. Item, when a steersman engages himself to a shipmaster, and it comes to pass that he is not good and competent for what he engaged for, so that the shipmaster's life and ship and the merchants' goods are endangered, it is ordained that such a steersman shall be given only half a mariner's hire and subsistence, provided the shipmaster can make good proof with two good men or with his crew that the steersman was not good enough for what he engaged himself.

"VI. Item, likewise, when a mariner engages himself with a shipmaster, and he is not good enough for what he engaged himself, to such a mariner shall be given no more than half the hire and half the subsistence, provided the shipmaster can prove it as above.

"VII. Item, when a steersman or mariner deserts the shipmaster, taking the wages that have been given him, it is ordained that, if such person be found, he shall in the first place restore his hire to the shipmaster, and such offence, the first time, shall be punished by the town [authorities] or judge where he is prosecuted, in discretion, according to the circumstances and occasion. If he does it a second time, then he shall be publicly flogged. But if he is found to do it for the third time, then he shall be punished capitally.

"VIII. Item, if any mariners happen to be such rascally evil-doers and have laid off, and united against the shipmaster, so as to mutiny against him with evil intent and thus to force him, it is ordained that in the first place he shall give back his hire to the shipmaster, and also he shall for the first offence be publicly beaten with rods in the pillory. And if he is found to have done it again, he shall be punished capitally.

"IX. Item, the Towns have resolved that if any steersman or mariner, while at sea, make any evil plots against the shipmaster without need or notable necessity to enter a port where he should not go, so that the shipmaster or merchant suffer damage or loss thereby, or desert the shipmaster without his will and authority, it is ordained that he shall be punished capitally.

"X. [Shipmasters who embezzle and abscond are to be punished capitally.]

"XI. Item, since the customs as to subsistence are doubtful and not uniform, it is ordained the mariners shall be allowed in grain two 'lasts' [180 bushels] for seven men, and in liquid goods four casks each.

"XI *bis*. Item, the mariners shall be obliged and bound, on penalty of forfeiting their subsistence, to shift the wheat as often as the shipmaster decides and orders; for every 'last' they shift, and as often as they shift, they shall have one 'plack', and for shaking the straw mats one groschen for every 'last'.

"XII. Item, if it happens that a shipmaster has loaded for a distant voyage and the shipmaster must by some event of necessity lay up the ship in dock before completing the voyage, and the merchants and the ship's friends decide that the shipmaster must nevertheless then continue the voyage, and the crew will not so continue, it is ordained that they shall not be given either hire or subsistence before the time that the voyage is completed.

"XIII. [Mariners must assist in case of shipwreck].

"XIV. [Mariners must not go ashore without the master's consent].

"XV. [Mariners' misbehavior prior to sailing].

"XVI. [Mariners' full hire payable if discharged before end of voyage].

"XVII. [Mariner injured when drunk ashore cannot claim his keep; otherwise when injured in the course of duty].

"XVIII. [Mariner too ill to stay on board must be furnished keep and attendance on shore].

"XIX. [Mariner misbehaving may be discharged].

"XX. [Harbor-pilot's duties].

"XXI. [Mariners must aid in repulsing pirates].

"XXII. [Shipmaster failing to resist pirates may be black-listed].

"XXIII. [Master or crew may not accept new position till voyage ended].

"The foregoing is publicly proclaimed on Saturday after Holy Cross Day in the year 1482."

These sea-laws, then, came into being from three sources,—from case-judgments of the local courts, from unofficial treatise-compilations by anonymous scribes, and from deliberate legislation by the sea-guilds. Their common feature was that they represented the customary law of the great community of sea-traders, distinct from any local territorial law of prince or baron.

(II) THE NATIONAL LAWS OF THE SEA

11. But with the period of the 1600's a new stage is entered. As time went on, and nations were being organized, this unique common law of the sea was breaking up. The 1600's was the period of nationalization of law all over

[*914*]

Europe. The growing sense of nationality was beginning to centralize, unify, and codify, in the name of the royal governments, all the diverse jurisdictions (princes, barons, bishops, cities, guilds) which had hitherto shared in parcels the power of legislation and justice. It was the same movement that in the same epoch was disintegrating and absorbing the Common Papal law (*post*, Chap. XIV) and the Common Romanesque law (*post*, Chap. XV) into the individual national laws. The sea-customs underwent with the rest this process of nationalization.

The process had begun indeed, in the prior century, in Denmark, with Frederic II's Maritime Code of 1561. But it now culminated simultaneously in Denmark, Sweden, and France,—in Sweden with the Maritime Code of Christian XI, in 1667; in France with Louis XIV's Marine Ordinance of 1681; and in Denmark with Christian V's Code of 1683, containing a book on Maritime Law.

Of these, the most influential was that of France, prepared under the great minister Colbert[27] as a part of his comprehensive plan for the nationalization and codification of all French law (*post*, Chap. XV). Colbert's Marine Ordinance, a masterpiece of lucid draftsmanship, based itself on the established customs of the sea, as handed down in the books of customs (revised to suit the

[*915*]

XIII. 27—Colbert, Minister of France
Legislator of the Marine Ordinance of 1681

times). But it now made them French law and enforced them in a royal court of justice,—the admiral's; giving to this court a monopoly of jurisdiction, and ousting the ancient courts of the consuls, elected by the men of the sea.[28] The new national spirit is embodied in the opening clauses:[e]

"I. 1. Justice shall be done in the name of the admiral in all courts of the admiralty.

"2. Nomination of all officers of the court . . . . . shall belong to the admiral. . . . . . .

"II. 2. The jurisdiction of the judges of the admiralty shall include . . . . . all actions concerning the commerce of the sea, notwithstanding any agreement or charter to the contrary . . . .

ORDONNANCE

DE LA MARINE,

DU MOIS D'AOUT 1681.

LOUIS, PAR LA GRACE DE DIEU, ROI DE FRANCE ET DE NAVARRE, à tous presens et à venir, salut. Après diverses ordonnances que nous avons faites, pour régler par de bonnes lois l'administration de la justice et de nos finances

XIII. 28—THE FRENCH MARINE ORDINANCE OF 1681

[*917*]

"15. We forbid all . . . . . . consul-judges . . . . . to take cognizance of any of the above-named cases,. . . . Likewise we forbid all merchants, mariners, and others to bring such causes before them, on penalty of a fine in discretion."

So ended, for France, the common law of the sea and the consular courts of the mariners. Other nations one by one followed in this path,—Holland, in 1721, by the Marine Ordinance of Rotterdam; Prussia, in 1727, by a Marine Ordinance; Spain, in 1737, by the Ordinances of Bilbao; Venice, in 1786, by the Code of Mercantile Marine. In England, between the 1600's and the 1800's, the local sea-courts had been gradually abolished (for some of them tenaciously opposed the tendency), and their jurisdiction was transferred to the admiralty and other national courts. By the 1800's the various national Codes of Commerce, following at intervals the French Code of 1807, had incorporated the maritime ordinances as one of the books within the general codes.

The common law of the sea had disappeared, apparently forever.

(III) THE COMMON LAW OF THE SEA, ONCE MORE

12. But the close of the 1800's saw its resurrection in a new form. A map shows the two hundred and twenty-two seaports of the world that were served in 1923 by the vessels under the United States Shipping Board alone;[29] the

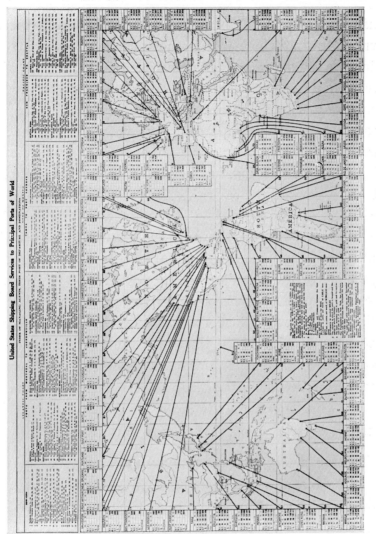

XIII. 29—Map of the United States Shipping Board Ports, 1923

square boxes on the margin show the hundred chief ports. Multiply these world sea-connections by twenty to include the other countries, and one gains some idea of present-day sea-commerce. Sea-transportation has been revolutionized in the past half century. This came about through the advent of steam for transportation and electricity for communication. It affected all stages of shipping,—the building, loading, routing, and unloading, the bill of lading, the sea-risks, the crew, the navigation rules, the harbor-customs, the wharfage, the banking, the brokerage, the terms of sale, and above all the insurance. And all of these distinct but related interests have been more or less standardized by powerful associations whose viewpoint has become international rather than national. The economic conditions of sea-commerce have changed more since 1830 than in all the two thousand years preceding. So that, once more, the maritime group —consisting now chiefly of ship-owners, merchants, and insurers—has found that it is united by vital common interests, overriding the diversity of national laws.

The movement for international uniformity began in the field of insurance against sea-loss,—general average; and a series of conferences resulted in the so-called York-Antwerp Rules of 1890, which codified that subject. The Hague Conference of 1921[30] was the later culmination of

12. Hague Rules of 1921

XIII. 30—THE HAGUE CONFERENCE OF 1921

these many forces. Two permanent unofficial bodies, one known as the International Maritime Committee, with branches in many nations, founded at Antwerp in 1897, and the other known as the International Law Association, had been engaged for fifty years in codifying once more the customs of the sea into a single universal body of rules. The codes thus far framed cover general average, ship's liability, ship's mortgage, and carrier's contract. The committees call a conference every year or so in Europe. The most important modern meeting was at the Hague in 1921; American delegates took part; and here

[*921*]

XIII. 31—THE HAGUE RULES IN SIX LANGUAGES

the codification of the carrier's contract was achieved. Its provisions became known as the Hague Rules of 1921.

Naturally the agreement of this powerful body on any set of rules amounts to a compulsory rule of mercantile custom for the individual merchant; for when a bill of lading founded on these rules is offered to him, he must accept it, or practically retire from the trade. The text of the Hague Rules, as adopted at the Conference, has been printed in six other great maritime languages,—French, Spanish, Italian, Dutch, German, Norwegian.[31] To ship-owners, shippers, and insurers all over the world they are available in the language of each country; so that they are genuinely international and world-wide. These Hague Rules have now begun to be used in export bills of lading; a bill of 1922, for example, incorporates the Hague Rules in the very first clause; and another clause invokes the entire eighteen articles of the York-Antwerp rules of 1890.[32]

13. Whether these rules will ever become formal law, in all nations, by treaty or national legislation, cannot be prophesied positively. England in 1924 had already enacted some of them. But it is plain that the world has entered upon a new third stage of internationally codified maritime law. This bill of lading, containing the clause just shown, will take a cargo literally around the world, to any of a score of nations, on the terms codified in the document, and virtually independent of any one nation's

LONDON to NEW YORK, U.S.A.—"Local."

Shipped in apparent good order and condition by..

at the port of **LONDON**, on board the...

the goods or packages of merchandise stated to be marked, numbered and described in this bill of lading (measure, brand, contents, quality and value unknown), to be

conveyed and delivered to...

or assigns, at **NEW YORK, U.S.A.** (or as near thereto as she may safely get), **Freight, Charges and Primage payable at**.......... ....

AND IT IS MUTUALLY AGREED AS FOLLOWS:—

1. **THE HAGUE RULES :**—This Bill of Lading is subject to The Hague Rules, 1921, and the Carrier shall also be entitled to claim and shall have the full benefit of all limitations of and exemptions from liability conferred on the Carrier and/or the ship by Public Law.

9. **GENERAL AVERAGE :**—General Average shall be payable according to York/Antwerp Rules, 1890, and Antwerp Rule, 1903, and shall be adjusted at any port or place selected by the Carrier.

XIII. 32—THE HAGUE RULES IN A BILL OF LADING

CONTRACT TERMS AND CONDITIONS

PART I.—With respect to the service until delivery at the port (A) first above mentioned it is agreed that—

PART II.—With respect to the service after delivery at the port (A) first above mentioned, and until delivery at the port (B) second above mentioned, it is agreed that—

PART III.—With respect to the service after delivery at the port (B) second above mentioned, and until delivery at ultimate destination if destined beyond that port, it is agreed that—

XIII. 33—A Round-the-World Bill of Lading, 1924

law.[33] So that a common law of the sea, based on the custom of merchants, is once more returning.

And the national legislatures may now with truth repeat almost the words of the Emperor Antoninus, nearly two thousand years ago, quoted already at the beginning of this chapter: "*We* are indeed the supreme lords of our lands. But Custom is the universal law of the sea".

XIII. Maritime Legal System

Sources of Illustrations

1. *Queen Hatsheput's Ship, B. C. 1500, in Egypt.* From a photograph, by *J. W. Butcher*, London, of the relief in the British Museum.

2. *Colonies of the Mediterranean, B. C. 500.* From the map in *Octave Noel*, "Histoire de la commerce du monde", vol. I (Paris, Plon, 3 vols. 1891).

3. *A Greek Five-Banked Galley.* From the illustration in "Bilder-Atlas", vol. IV, plate 1, fig. 1 (Leipzig, Brockhaus, 1875).

4. *Roman Digest; The Lex Rhodia.* From the facsimile reproduction of Digesta, XIV, 2, 9, in the Florentine MS., ed. Krüger and Mommsen, in the Laurentian Library at Florence.

5. *Colossus at Rhodes.* From the painting by *J. F. Kapkoff*, as reproduced in *J. A. Hammerton*, "Wonders of the Past", vol. III, p. 676 (New York, Putnam, 1924).

6. *Amalfi, from the Sea.* From a photograph by *E. Ragozino*, Galleria Umberto, Naples.

7. *Code of Amalfi.* From the reprint in *N. Alianelli*, "Antichi Consuetudini e Leggi Marittimi della Principalità di Napoli", p. 101 (Naples, 1871).

8. *Judgment of the Council of Ten.* From a collection of the originals (obtained at Venice in 1923) in the Elbert H. Gary Library of Law of Northwestern University.

9. *Gate of Placards.* From a photograph by Fratelli *Alinari*, Venice.

10. *Chamber of the Inquisitors.* From a photograph by Fratelli *Alinari*, Venice.

11. *Bank of St. George.* From a photograph by *Carlo Paganini*, Genoa.

12. *Barcelona.* From the drawing in *E. H. Locker*, "Views in Spain", No. 60 (London, Murray, 1824).

13. *Consulado del Mar, MS.* From a photograph furnished by *Lecuyer*, Paris, of the original in the Bibliothèque Nationale (fol. 1, verso, MS. Espagnol 124).

14. *Consulado*, in Catalan. From the edition of 1523, published at Barcelona.

15. *Consolato*, in Italian. From the edition of 1566, published at Venice.

16. *Consolato*, in Dutch. From the edition of 1704, published at Amsterdam.

17. *Island of Oleron.* From a photograph by *R. Bergevini*, Bordeaux, furnished by Prof. *Léon Duguit*, of the University of Bordeaux.

Sources

18. *Laws of Oleron*, MS. From the facsimile in Sir *Travers Twiss*, "Black Book of the Admiralty", vol. I, frontispiece (London, 1871).

19. *Oak Book of Southampton*. From the illustration in *P. Studer*, "The Oak Book of Southampton", vol. I, frontispiece (Southampton Record Society, F. J. C. Hearnshaw, general editor, 1910).

20. *Wisby's Gate*. From the illustration in *Wm. E. Curtis*, "Denmark, Sweden, and Norway", pp. 480, 489 (Akron, Ohio, Saalfield Publishing Co., 1903).

21. *Hansa Yard at Bergen, Norway*. From a view furnished by *Ben Blossum*, Agent for the Norwegian State Railways, New York (1925).

22. *The Steelyard, London*. From the illustration in *G. W. Thornbury*, "Old and New London", vol. I, p. 31 (London, Cassell, 1873-1886).

23. *Town Council House at Lübeck*. From the illustration in *Helen Zimmern*, "The Hansa Towns", p. 367 (New York, Putnam, 1891).

24. *Hansa Shipping Ordinance*. From the "Lübeck Statuta und Stadt Recht", p. 83 (Lübeck, 1657).

25. *Map of the Shift of Maritime Codes*. Prepared by the author.

26. *Hansa Fleet's Home-coming at Lübeck*. From a lithograph of the painting by *Felix Schwarmstädt*, obtained in Lübeck for the author by *Einar Söderval* of Chicago.

27. *Colbert*. From the same source as in Chapter XV.

28. *Ordonnance de la Marine*. From *Becane's* edition of *Valin's* "Commentaire sur l'Ordonnance de la Marine", p. 1 (Poitiers, 1829).

29. *Map of the United States Shipping Board*. From a publication of the Board, January 1923.

30. *Hague Conference of 1921*. From the frontispiece to the "Proceedings of the Thirtieth Conference of the International Law Association", at the Peace Palace, the Hague, 1921.

31. *The Hague Rules in Six Languages*. From the "Proceedings" (above cited), p. 255.

32. *The Hague Rules in a Bill of Lading*. From a B. L. of the Furness Line, No. 10843 (1922), furnished by *Charles S. Haight*, Esq., of New York.

33. *Round-the-World Bill of Lading*. From a B. L. of the Canadian Pacific Co., Form 1227, Correction 3.

XIII. Maritime Legal System

Sources of Documents Quoted in Text

a. Passage from the Consulado del Mar. From the translation in *Twiss*, "Black Book of the Admiralty" (cited *infra*), vol. III, p. 187.

b. Passage from the Ordinance of Valencia. From the French translation in *P. B. Boucher*, "Consulat de la Mar", vol. II, p. 1 (Paris, 1801).

c. Judgments of local sea-courts. There are indeed some interesting records (complaints, answers, arbitrators' decisions) of disputes between the towns in the proceedings of the Hansa Assemblies (e. g. "Hanse-Recesse", cited *infra*, 1st ser., vol. I, No. 141, No. 161, No. 211, and "Hansisches Urkundenbuch", vol. VIII, Nos. 110, 111, 164-167, 1150, 1255) and occasionally these disputes concerned matters of sea-law ("Hanse-Recesse", *supra*, Nos. 548-554). But these were rather quasi-international negotiations, in which the officers of one town or nation made claim against those of another for wrongs suffered by the individual citizens of one at the hands of those of the other.

In Alianelli's "Leggi Marittimi" (cited *supra*), at p. 89, a footnote reports that in the Naples newspaper "La Patria" of April 9, 1870, someone announces that "at the forthcoming International Maritime Exposition will be shown a book containing a collection of unpublished judgments of the court of admiralty of Amalfi". This would indeed be a treasure,—the earliest sea-judgments extant. But inquiries in qualified quarters have thus far failed to locate the book.

d. Hansa Ordinance of 1482. Translated from the old German in *Dietrich Schäfer*, ed. "Hanse-Recesse", 3d ser., vol. I, Nos. 317, 318, 334, 357, 365, 367 (Leipzig, 1881); the ordinance-text is also translated into French in *Pardessus* (cited *infra*), II, 497.

e. Passage from the Ordonnance de la Marine. From the French text in Becane's edition of Valin's Commentary (cited *supra*), p. 2.

General References

W. S. *Holdsworth*, "A History of English Law", vol. I, book I, ch. VII; vol. V, pp. 60-154, "Commercial and Maritime Law" (London, Methuen, 1924).

F. L. *Mears*, "History of the Admiralty Jurisdiction", in "Select Essays in Anglo-American Legal History", vol. II, p. 312 (1908).

"Progress of Continental Law in the Nineteenth Century" (Continental Legal History Series, vol. XI), chapters by G. *Ripert*, "Unification of Maritime Law", and G. *Cohn*, "International Assimilation of Commercial Law" (Boston, Little, Brown & Co., 1918).

Sources

Arthur Desjardins, "Introduction historique a l'étude du droit Commercial Maritime" (Paris, Pedone-Lauriel, 1890).

Sir *Travers Twiss*, "The Black Book of the Admiralty", giving in original text and translations all the chief sea-codes (London, 4 vols. 1874; published under the Master of the Rolls, as part of the "Monumenta Juridica" of "Rerum Britannicarum Medii Aevi Scriptores").

J. M. Pardessus, "Collection des Lois Maritimes" (6 vols., Paris, 1828-45; giving in original text and French translation the principal monuments of sea-law; a rare work, almost never coming on the market).

H. Zeller, "Sammlung älterer Seerechtsquellen" (in serial parts, Mainz, 1906+; giving the original text and the translation).

Walter Ashburner, "The Rhodian Sea-Law" (Oxford, 1909).

L. Goldschmidt, "Handbuch des Handelsrechts, 1ste Abth., Universal-geschichte des Handelsrechts", §11, "Das Seerecht" (Stuttgart, 1891).

Helen Zimmern, "The Hansa Towns" (New York, Putnam, 1891).

THE
PAPAL
LEGAL SYSTEM

XIV

The Papal (or Canon) Legal System

1. The early claim of universal jurisdiction for St. Peter's successor—Extension of the Church's rule from the Balkans to Greenland.

2. The judicial and legislative system—The Cardinal Chancellor—The Sacra Romana Rota—An Opinion by Coccinus—The Consistory and the Congregations.

3. Compilation of the recorded sources—The Decretum of Gratian—The rise of Canon Law as a system—Doctor Johannes Andreae.

4. The Decretals of Pope Gregory IX—A Decretal invalidating a usurious mortgage—A Decretal regulating criminal procedure.

5. The Corpus Juris Canonici—Pope Innocent III, the great legislator—Culmination of the Church's sway under Innocent III.

6. The Church courts—Their extensive and progressive influence—St. Ives, the Church judge and patron saint of the legal profession.

7. Rise of nationalism undermines the Church's political authority—The Council of Trent—The statutes of Henry VIII—Absorption of the Papal jurisdiction by national courts and legislatures.

8. Codification of the Papal Regulations in 1917—The Codex Juris Canonici.

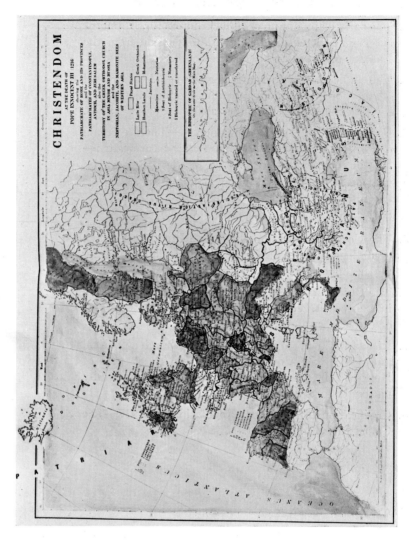

XIV. 1—Map Showing the Papal Jurisdiction A. D. 1200
The shadings represent merely various subdivisions

XIV

The Papal (or Canon) Legal System

THE Bishop of Rome was early recognized as the successor of Saint Peter, whose bronze statue stands in the Vatican. That Bishop under Latin Christianity was given the title of Pontifex Maximus, a title already familiar in the pagan priesthood. And, in the course of time, the successor of Saint Peter began to claim universal jurisdiction of law, not only over the Christian Church, but also over temporal kings and princes. The typical expression of this claim is found in a supposed letter of Pope Clement I, A. D. 91, addressed to the clergy, and later included in the so-called Decretals of Isidore; the vital clauses read:[a]

"Your duty is to teach the peoples. Their duty is to obey you as they would God Himself. . . . And all princes, high or low, and other peoples, tribes, and languages, who do not obey shall be infamous, and shall be cast out from the kingdom of God and the company of the faithful."

These words described during some centuries the dominance of the church's supreme jurisdiction over morals and faith. This quasi-Federal jurisdiction of the church had its own tribunals (like the American Federal ones) for its own special field, alongside the other courts; but it claimed and received a supreme appellate political jurisdiction over all temporal kings and kingdoms, with the Pope as Pontifex Maximus, judging all men, and judged by none.

From Serbia on the east to Iceland and Greenland on the northwest extended the jurisdiction of this theocracy.[1] Its sway was at the zenith in the centuries A. D. 800-1200; it ended by four hundred years later, and it had begun four hundred years earlier,—twelve centuries in all.

The early papal letter of A. D. 91, above quoted, dating this charter of supremacy back to early Christianity,[2] was

XIV. 2—LETTER OF POPE CLEMENT I
"The peoples' duty is to obey you as they would God Himself"

XIV. 3—Palace of the Cancelleria

false, the words having been forged (long after that date) by an obscure medieval monk, as was discovered many centuries later. Nevertheless, as early as A. D. 400 Pope Damasus had begun to claim papal supremacy; and the Roman Emperor Valentinian III, in a decree of A. D. 445,[b] had acknowledged the claim of Leo I, Bishop of Rome, to be the supreme judge, at least over the universal church.

2. Today, in Rome, at the very spot of earth where Pope Damasus, fifteen centuries ago, once held his court of justice with pomp and ceremony, stands the superb Palace of the Cancelleria, or Papal Chancery.[3] This is the office of the Cardinal Chancellor of the papal church; he is the most powerful dignitary next to the Pontiff himself; he carries the sceptre of justice, and signs all papal decrees issued under the famous lead-seal (technically known as "bull").

In a more modest chamber meets the once supreme civil tribunal of the papal church, the Sacra Romana Rota, or Holy Roman Wheel.[4] This court was termed, "Totius Christiani orbis supremum tribunale", "the supreme tribunal of the whole Christian world". In its most flourishing period, the 1400's and 1500's, it was deemed (in the words of a modern German scholar) "the most eminent and weighty court in the world." The

[*937*]

meetings of the Rota were (and are still) held in private. The tribunal was called Rota, or wheel, because (as some say) originally its judges sat around a table in a circle, or, because cases were assigned in rotation to each judge. Its jurisdiction being so extensive and cosmopolitan, its membership (finally fixed at twelve) was required to represent the varied regions within the church's fold; the allotment was: three from Rome, two from Spain, and one each from Germany, France, Venice, Milan, Ferrara, Tuscany, and Bologna. Emperors and kings once brought their

XIV. 4—CHAMBER OF THE SACRA ROMANA ROTA
This photograph was taken in 1923, by special permission
of the Papal authorities

causes to the tribunal of the Rota; but since the loss of the church's temporal power, the Rota's jurisdiction has become a minor one.

Hundreds of tomes now form the six centuries' accumulation of the Rota's opinions. Usually they were published as the collected opinions of some individual judge. Penia and Coccinus were eminent Deans of the Rota in its palmier days,[5] the former in the 1500's, the latter in the 1600's. John Baptist Coccinus held that high office for twenty-eight years; his opinions numbered about fifty a year. They are seldom lengthy; and the following one, from the first of his five large volumes, is typical of their style (the headnotes are by the judge's editor, and they reveal that the art of elaborate headnotes is no invention of the modern reporter):[c]

[*An Opinion of Coccinus, Dean of the Rota.*] "Rome: The Bull 'Juris Congrui'.

"Monday, 5 June 1600.

"*Topic:* The owner of a plot or house, intending to build, is not compellable to sell by virtue of the Bull 'Juris Congrui'.

"*Summary:* 1. No one against his will is compelled to sell. 2. The owner of an estate, intending to build, has priority over others wishing to build. 3. The Bull 'Juris Congrui' declares only the general principle that an owner may be compelled to sell against his will. 4. When a remedial measure could have one or two effects contrary to existing law, it is always to be interpreted so as to do least change to the common law. 5. Size and proximity of

XIV. 5—Penia and Coccinus
Former Deans of the Rota, i. e. Chief Justices of the Supreme Court

premises are immaterial in building by the common law; otherwise, by the terms of the Bull 'Juris Congrui'. 6. For the owner not willing to sell, but intending to build, a time-limit should be set for his building."

"*Opinion.* John James Ferrari, alleging that he wished to build for the beautification of the city, petitioned for the sale to him, pursuant to the Bull 'Juris Congrui', of an adjacent building of the German College; the College replied that it also intended to build for the beautification of the city, to the full area of its ground.

"The case being submitted to me from the Rota, I doubted whether the said James could compel the College to sell the said house. And the other members of the Rota were of opinion that the College was not compellable. The ground of this opinion was a former decision of 15 June 1579 [citing the reference]. For in law there are two distinct and fundamental principles in favor of owners: [1] one is that no one is against his will compellable to sell (lex 'dudum', statute 'de contrahenda emptione'); [2] the other is, that in equal circumstances an owner has priority over all other persons wishing to do the same thing (lex 'si cum dotem', § finalis, ss. 'solutis matrimoniis', lex 'ex facto', ss. 'de peculio', Caputaquis, Decisio 99).

"[3] Hence, this Bull, which declares only the general principle that an owner *may* be compelled to sell, contrary to lex 'invictam' and the above-cited lex 'dudum' in the statute 'de contrahenda emptione', alters the common law on that point only, and on others, not covered by it, must be deemed to refer to the common law and to receive from the same its interpretation. For [4] when a remedial measure could have one or two effects contrary to existing law, it is always to be interpreted so as to have one effect only and to do least change to the common law [citing authorities]. And therefore the Bull does not change the common law that when an owner, here the College, intends to build, he cannot be compelled to sell.

[*941*]

"[5] The greater area and proximity of the land to Ferrari, etc., is immaterial; those circumstances would be material if the case came within the above statute; but do not affect the result here, where we are governed by the rules of common law.

"[6] Nor does it suffice to argue that the statute is rendered elusory by our decision because the owner [whose land is sought] could always set up that he intended to build; for a time-limit must be set for such building, after the lapse of which this house may be proceeded against, according to the form of the said statute."

Most cases of church litigation are now dealt with by a Committee of the Cardinals, known as the Congregation of the Council, because it interprets the fundamental laws passed by the Council of Trent, the last universal church assembly. This Congregation now has its office in the Palace of the Chancery, already shown.

The supreme advisory legislative tribunal used to be the Consistory of Cardinals, or Senate of the Church, the Pontiff presiding; sometimes a Consistory was held in the Sistine Chapel, with Michael Angelo's world-famous fresco on the wall over the altar.[6] But the Consistory now reserves for itself only matters of highest moment, and delegates its various powers to the Congregations, or Committees, already mentioned.

3. The legislation and decisions of the Popes, after accumulating for seven centuries in thousands of separate decrees, rescripts, bulls, and council-resolutions, were first

XIV. 6—A Consistory in the Sistine Chapel

systematically digested in the so-called Decretum of
Gratian,—a private compilation made about A. D. 1140,
by an obscure monk named Gratian, at the University of
Bologna.⁷ Twice in history the growth of the papal
supreme jurisdiction received a powerful impulse from
literature; the first impulse was given by the forged
Decretals of Isidore, in the 800's, already mentioned; and
now it took place a second time, in this Decretum,—one
of those great text-books which by appearing just at the
right time and the right place, becomes universally
revered as equal to law. Gratian's huge labors of search
and sorting brought clarity out of chaos, and now first
made these materials available for ready reference by all.
The Decretum virtually created Canon (or papal) law as
an independent system. Exalting the papal authority, it
met papal favor. The Emperors were favoring the then
recently resurrected imperial law of Rome (*post*, Chap.
XV); and so the Popes, in their rivalry with the Emperors,
welcomed the strong legal support found in the Decretum.

Canon law now began to be taught in the newly
arisen universities (*post*, Chap. XV), alongside of the
Roman law of Justinian; and the degree of J. U. D.
("juris utriusque doctor") came into use as signifying a
master who had compassed both branches of law. The
tombs of these doctors of Canon law show that their fame

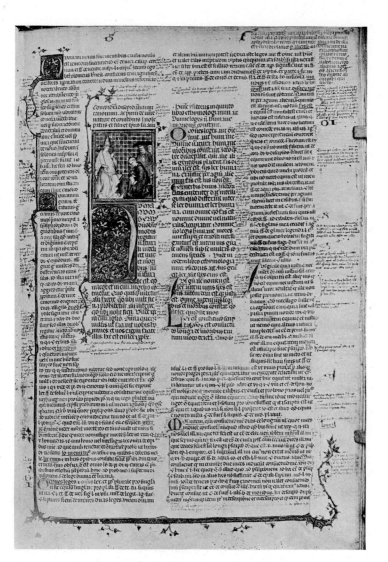

XIV. 7—Decretum Gratiani
This compilation virtually created Canon, or Papal, Law
as an independent system

[945]

XIV. 8—Tomb of Johannes Andreae, Doctor of Canon Law

[946]

equaled that of the other branch. One of the most eminent, Johannes Andreae,[8] a professor at the University of Bologna, in the early 1300's, was so well-beloved in Bologna that when the University by an ordinance forbade any member of the University to become godfather to any family of Bologna citizens, it made a special exception in favor of Andreae and all his descendants forever. Andreae bestowed upon his youngest and favorite daughter the name "Ordi-nancy" ("Novella"); and she is recorded to have been so learned in the law that sometimes in his absence she occupied his chair and lectured on the Canon law—but behind a curtain, lest her beauty distract the students' attention!

4. Gratian's Decretum was given official sanction by Pope Gregory IX, in the next century, A. D. 1234, by an extensive supplement, known as the Decretalia, or Decretals.[9] This new work, the Decretals, was an official compilation, and was required to be taught in all universities. It was prepared, under direction of the Legislator-Pope Gregory IX, by Raymond of Pennafort, one of the judges of the Rota, or Supreme Court. In point of system, it marked a decided advance on Gratian's work; its two thousand paragraphs were arranged in books, titles, and chapters (really, sections), under a more

XIV. 10—DECRETALS OF POPE GREGORY IX

XIV. 9—Pope Gregory IX Issuing the Decretals

synthetic classification,—a forerunner of our modern digests.[10]

The following passages illustrate the materials used:[d]

[*The Decretals; Book III, Title XVII.*] "Sale and purchase: *Chap. I* (Resolution of the Council at Valencia):

"It was resolved, by us and our faithful associates, that the elders admonish their people that they be hospitable and do not refuse lodging to any traveler, and that, to remove all chance of extortion, they do not sell at higher price to the passer-by than they could sell in the market; and that the passer-by, if not so treated, report to the elder, so that by his order they may sell humanely."

. . . .

[*Ibid, Chap. V.*] Innocent III to the Bishop of Pallia [A. D. 1203]: "It has lately come to our hearing, when R. a layman sought a loan from M., that the creditor, a man of the diocese of Trani, lest he be later brought into conflict with the canon against usury, received some houses and olive-groves of the said R. under terms of a sale, although the transaction was in fact an usurious contract, which appears plainly from the circumstance (set forth in the notarial instrument) that the creditor promised the debtor that he would restore the houses and olive-groves whenever between the seventh and ninth years thereafter the debtor should pay forty ounces of Tarenian money, which amount to scarce one-half the fair value. Therefore, since fraud cannot be condoned in any one, we order your fraternity, by virtue of the apostolic scriptures, that if the facts are as above, viz. the deed of sale was executed in evasion of the canon against usury, you compel the said M., under penalty as prescribed by the Lateran Council against usury, to restore the said houses and olive-groves to him to whom they may now belong by inheritance, the borrower himself having perhaps now gone the way of all flesh."

[*949*]

And the following passage has a deep intrinsic interest for the modern lawyer, even yet; for this Canon formed the main starting-point for the church's method of criminal prosecution—the so-called "ex officio" or inquisitorial method—which set the model for all later Continental procedure, in contrast with the old Germanic "accusatory" method—the method of individual complaint—which survived in England until modern times:

[*The Decretals: Book V, Title I.*] Prosecutions: Chap. XXIV. Innocent III, in General Council at the Lateran [A. D. 1215]: "How and when a prelate should proceed to investigate and punish the offences of his subordinates is plainly to be gathered from the authorities of the old and the new Testaments, on which later the canonical sanctions were founded, as we have already publicly pointed out, and which we now confirm by authority of the holy Council. For it is written in the gospel that the steward, who was reputed to his master to have squandered the estate, heard these words from the master: 'How is it that I hear this of thee? Give an account of thy stewardship, for thou mayest no longer be steward'. And in Genesis the Lord said [of Gomorrah], 'I will go down and see whether they have done altogether as the cry which comes to me'. From which authorities it is plainly proved that, not only when a subordinate, but also when a prelate has sinned, if it has come to the ears of his superior by clamor and repute [clamorem et famam]— not indeed of the malicious and loose-tongued but of the serious and honorable, nor once only but often, which the clamor and the repute will show—then the truth should be diligently inquired into before the elders of the church. . . . The party should be present, against whom the inquisition is to be made (unless he contumaciously absents himself). The items of charge, on which the inquiry is to be made are to be explained to him, so that he have opportunity to defend himself. And not only the sayings, but also the very names of the witnesses are to be made known, so that it may appear what was said and by whom. Nor are his lawful impeachments and rebuttals of them to be rejected, lest by suppressing the names of the detractors or not listening to the grounds of impeachment encouragement be given to bold defamers. . . . . . . Now as there are three methods of proceeding, viz. by complaint, by information, and by interrogation [inquisitio] of the parties themselves, nevertheless diligent caution must be used in all three of them, lest a too ready haste result in grave injustice; so the method of lawful complaint [by an injured party] must be preceded by a written statement; the method of information must be preceded by an earnest warning [to the informer]; and the method of inquisition by a clamorous rumor [clamosa insinuatio]."

These two works, the Decretum and the Decretalia, with some later supplements, were edited in A. D. 1582 (after the reformatory legislation of the Council of Trent, A. D. 1563), at the command of Gregory XIII, by a commission of six cardinals and fifteen doctors of law, and this compilation was officially entitled "Corpus Juris Canonici". This work, in various printed editions, remained the universal basis of papal law into modern times, until a few years ago. To the law up to the time of Gratian's Decretum was commonly given the epithet "jus antiquum"; to the ensuing law up to the Council of Trent, "jus novum"; and to the later law, "jus novissimum".

5. But the real credit for the great compilation of Gregory IX must be given to another papal legislator, the

most famous one—Pope Innocent III, who died A. D.
1216, just before the Decretals of Pope Gregory appeared.
Innocent III was a prolific legislator; in his reign of
eighteen years he had himself issued some thirty-four
hundred decrees.[11]   Innocent III had planned to systema-

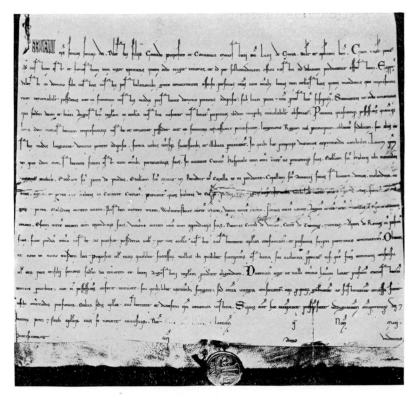

XIV. 11—A BULL OF INNOCENT III

This decree, or bull, is a grant confirming a monastery in its possessions.   The leaden seal ("bulla") is seen at the bottom

XIV. 12—POPE INNOCENT III

tize the church's enormous accumulation of law; but he did not live to execute the plan.

It must be remembered, in speaking of him as legislator and judge, that Innocent represented, in legal theory, a one-man autocracy. Even at the present day, when the Roman church is politically only a religious group, Catholic jurists speak of the Roman pontiff as "the supreme teacher, law-giver, and judge" over the religious affairs of all within the faith. But in Innocent's day the Roman church was vastly more than that; it claimed and possessed supreme temporal political power over the entire Christian world. Rome was once more the mistress of Europe, and kings were its vassals. Its clergy were immune from the criminal justice of the state. Its legislation covered the whole of human existence from the cradle to the grave; it was upheld by penalties that neither the proudest monarch nor the humblest peasant could escape; and it was administered by a supreme world-judge responsible to no earthly superior for his actions.

Innocent III was perhaps the youngest man ever elected Pope, being then only thirty-seven years of age. The best portrait of him[12] shows the youthfulness of the face, which is in unique contrast to portraits of the other Popes. Innocent III was the ambitious and masterful autocrat who humbled the English King John for signing

[*953*]

Magna Carta, and who reduced England, for a short period, to be only a vassal of the papacy; he annulled Magna Carta, declaring it vile and base. In his day he named emperors and tamed kings. He excommunicated whole nations. He established the inquisition of heresy, by warrants extending into every corner of Europe,—a form of terrorism which served to extirpate those who dissented from the church's dogmas for the next four centuries; indeed, as late a date as 1793[13] is found on a mandate of the Holy Inquisition, chanced upon in Madrid; the mandate authorizes the Inquisitor to use "arms offensive and defensive", and makes him immune from interference by the regular courts.[e] It was a church court, presided over by the Pope's delegate, which tried for heresy Galileo Galilei,[14] the world's greatest scientist of the day, just three centuries ago; and it was a church court which later imprisoned him and threatened him with torture until he recanted his great scientific proposition that the earth moves around the sun and not the sun around the earth. It was a church court which tried for heresy one of the most heroic patriots in the world's history, Joan of Arc:[15] her devoted leadership had saved the French kingdom from dissolution; but after a trial lasting three months, regularly held by clericals under a warrant of inquisition for heresy, sitting in a

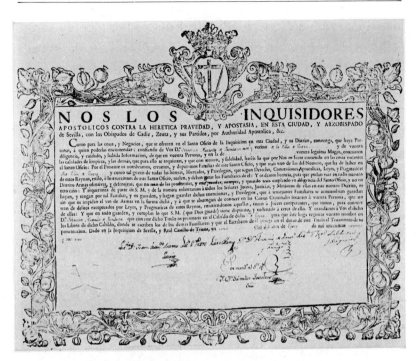

XIV. 13—A MANDATE OF THE HOLY INQUISITION
This was found in Madrid, and is dated A. D. 1793, long
after the disbanding of the Holy Office elsewhere

chapel, and presided over by a bishop, she was found guilty of heresy, and was later burned at the stake.

6. The church courts, it must be remembered, were, in those days, not only as important as the secular courts in the daily life of the peoples of Europe; but they rendered invaluable service to the cause of justice. Secular

justice, administered chiefly by hundreds of petty independent barons and princes, was local and weak, selfish and mercenary, crude and unprogressive (*ante*, Chap. XII). The church's law then represented the progressive and efficient methods of the period. The church forbade the irrational "trial by battle", or legal duel, which was still in common use in the secular courts. The church revolutionized criminal and civil procedure in western Europe; and the modern Anglican chancery practice can be traced directly back to Innocent III's institutions. The church laid the foundations of inter-

XIV. 14—GALILEO BEFORE THE INQUISITION

XIV. 15—TRIAL OF JOAN OF ARC

national law; for before men were ever Frenchmen or Englishmen they were Christians, and the modern so-called law of nations began by being a "jus inter christianos". The church's theory led up to the conception of the modern State as a power held in trust for the welfare of the nation, superseding the feudal idea of government as a property-right of the ruler. The church first in Europe laid down the modern principle of equality before the law; it protected the poor and the weak against the rich and the powerful.

A famous statue, showing the judge standing impartially between the rich man and the poor man,[16] represents Ivo, or St. Ives, an ecclesiastical judge in Brittany, of A. D. 1300, around whom cluster the most admirable traditions of our legal profession.

XIV. 16—STATUE OF ST. IVES

He stands between a rich magnate and a poor peasant, signifying equal justice for all

6. *The Church's Justice*

The statue stands on a pillar in the church in his native township of Tréguier, in Brittany. At Rome there is a chapel in honor of St. Ives; the inscription over the door calls him "advocatus pauperum", "the poor man's lawyer". Among the classical painters a favorite theme was St. Ives on his judicial bench receiving the petitions of children. He is the chosen saint for the University at Rome; in the chapel of the Sapienza ("Learning"; the old name for the University) a spacious mural painting depicts St. Ives, clad in

XIV. 17
ST. IVES ATTENDING TO THE PETITIONS OF THE POOR

This painting fills the chancel-wall of the chapel of the Sapienza (University) at Rome

his lawyer's robes, benevolently attending to the petitions of the poor[17]; and on his death-day, the 19th of May, each year a memorial mass is here celebrated. In Brittany his court was thronged with suppliants for justice; a favorite saying of his, when pronouncing judgment, was, "Bon droit et raison", "This is good law and equity". The popular verdict on his character shames the repute of our profession; for the saying ran, of him, "Advocatus sed non latro, res miranda populo", "He was a lawyer, yet not a rascal, and the people were astonished". On his death he was proposed for canonization as a saint; and every Faculty of Law in Europe, as well as a host of kings, barons, and lesser men, joined in the petition. He is reputed to be the only lawyer who was ever made a saint.[f]

His tomb, in the churchyard at Tréguier, in Brittany, is sought by pilgrims, hoping for his protection,[18] even at this day, six centuries later; the suppliants ensure

XIV. 18—PILGRIMS AT THE TOMB OF ST. IVES
The tomb is in the churchyard of St. Minihy, at
Tréguier, Brittany, his native place

6. *The Church's Justice*

XIV. 19—A Foreign Lawyer at the Tomb of St. Ives

their prayers by creeping on their knees through the arch of the saint's tombstone, and they confidently appeal to him to do justice and send retribution on their enemies. Even a foreign lawyer may sometimes be found making a pilgrimage to the grave of this patron saint of the legal profession,[19]—this humble judge of the church court, who once made the name of Law synonymous with Justice throughout Europe.

7. But meantime, as the thirteenth century ended, the principles of patriotic nationality and legislative independence were rising and growing slowly stronger through-

out the west of Europe. This movement dates notably from the time of Louis IX (known as St. Louis), king of France, famous for his personal interest in dispensing justice, and often depicted in that role.[20] And in England, the same rise of nationalism and unified legislation is marked by the reign of Edward I, about A. D. 1300; Edward, for his vigorous constructive influence on English national legislation, has been given the epithet (hardly appropriate) of "the English Justinian". And, so by the time of Luther, of Knox, and of Calvin, in the 1500's, the Universal Church was no longer a universal power.

In the Council Church at Trent, a city in the Tyrolean Alps (which has now become Italian territory once more) took place, in A. D. 1545, the last really Universal Church Council ever destined to assemble. It was attended by over three hundred bishops, ambassadors, cardinals, and other delegates. The great Titian made a painting of it, which now hangs in the Louvre.[21] The deliberations of the Council of Trent, with the adjournments, covered eighteen years, and its legislation ranged over the whole system of Canon law. But by the time this Council ended, the Protestant seceders had broken the church's universal power. The National secular law in each country of Europe was thenceforth to become supreme and exclusive.

[*962*]

XIV. 20—King Louis IX Dispensing Justice

XIV. 21—The Council of Trent

It was attended by over three hundred bishops, cardinals, ambassadors, and other delegates.
Its sessions (with adjournments) lasted for eighteen years

7. *Rise of Nationalism*

The temporal jurisdiction of the papal courts was in time abolished by the various national legislatures. In France, this took place by a series of statutes, beginning in the 1400's and culminating in a statute of the Revolutionary Assembly, in 1790, which abolished the church courts. But in England, the break had come suddenly and completely, by a group of statutes, in A. D. 1532-1534,—measures framed and demanded by King Henry VIII, but fully supported by popular opinion.[g] One statute forbade appeals from English soil to the justice of the Pope; another statute made the English church master of its own legislation, but subject to the king's approval; and a third declared the king to be "the only supreme head in earth of the church of England". The entire papal jurisdiction was transferred to the National courts.

The momentous legal significance of the break can be clearly realized in the rudely resolute and sweepingly self-assertive phrases of the statute of 25 Henry VIII:

[*Statute of 25 Henry VIII Nationalizing Church Law.*] "Whereas . . . . this realm of England, is an empire, and so hath been accepted in the world, governed by one supreme head and king, having the dignity and royal estate of the imperial crown of the same; unto whom a body politick, compact of all sorts and degrees of people, divided in terms and by names of spiritualty and temporalty, hath been bounden and owen to bear, next to God, a natural and humble obedience; he being also institute and furnished, by the goodness and sufferance of Almighty God, with plenary, whole, and entire power, pre-eminence, authority, prerogative and jurisdiction, to render and yield justice and final determination to all manner of folk, resiants, or subjects within this his realm, in all causes, matters, debates and contentions, happening to occur, insurge, or begin within the limits thereof, without restraint, or provocation to any foreign princes or potentates of the world. . . . . . .

"And whereas the king, his most noble progenitors, and the nobility and commons of this said realm, at divers and sundry parliaments . . . . . made sundry ordinances, laws, statutes, and provisions for the entire and sure conservation of the prerogatives, liberties and preëminences of the said imperial crown of this realm, and of the jurisdiction spiritual and temporal of the same, to keep it from the annoyance as well of the see of Rome, as from the authority of other foreign potentates, attempting the diminution or violation thereof. . . . . Yet nevertheless sithen the making of the said good statutes and ordinances, divers and sundry inconveniences and dangers, not provided for plainly by the said former acts, statutes and ordinances, have arisen and sprung by reason of appeals sued out of this realm to the see of Rome, in causes testamentary, causes of matrimony and divorces, right of tithes, oblations and obventions. . . . .

"In consideration whereof, the king's highness, his nobles and commons . . . . enact, establish and ordain, That all causes testamentary, causes of matrimony and divorces, rights of tithes, oblations and obventions . . . . already commenced, moved, depending, being, happening, or hereafter coming in contention, debate or question within this realm . . . . shall be from henceforth heard, examined, discussed, clearly, finally, and definitely adjudged and determined within the king's jurisdiction and authority, and not elsewhere . . . . any foreign inhibitions, appeals, sentences, summons, citations, suspensions, interdictions, excommunications, restraints, judgments, or any other process or impediments, of what natures, names, qualities, or conditions soever they be, from the see of Rome, or any other foreign courts or potentates of the world . . . . . . to the let or impediment thereof in any wise notwithstanding."

Then and there ended—for England—the system of papal ecclesiastical law; that is, as a body of law existing independently of the State, and enforced by an extra-national authority.

And so today the Codex Juris Canonici, the Papal Code of 1917, is, by its own terms, merely the Catholic Church's code of morals and discipline for its own believers.[h]

8. By the close of the nineteenth century, the huge mass of papal church-law stood in need of a thorough restatement. During the seven centuries since the Decretum and the Decretalia, thousands of ordinances of supplementary legislation had accumulated; manners and customs had changed; the temporal jurisdiction of the Pope had ended; new world-wide spiritual areas had been added; much of the law was obsolete; and much of the remainder was difficult to trace through the seven centuries of records.

A commission was therefore appointed, in 1904, by Pope Pius X. Its vast labors, which included consultation with clerical authorities all over the world, had

Cardinal Gasparri at the head of the commission, and were completed in twelve years; and on May 27, 1917, was promulgated by Pope Benedict XV the Codex Juris Canonici.[22]

This work, unlike the old Corpus Juris Canonici (with its Decretum, Decretalia, and Supplements), is not a compilation, but a genuine codification,—one of the modern world's greatest masterpieces of composition. Its text is in lucid Latin—the only near-universal language; its general style may be seen in the following passages:[i]

[*Codex Juris Canonici.*] "Can. 1553. §1. Ecclesia iure proprio et exclusivo cognoscit:

"(1) De causis quae respiciunt res spirituales et spiritualibus adnexas;

"(2) De violatione legum ecclesiasticarum deque omnibus in quibus inest ratio peccati, quod attinet ad culpae definitionem et poenarum ecclesiasticarum irrogationem;

"(3) De omnibus causis sive contentiosis sive criminalibus quae respiciunt personas privilegio fori gaudentes ad norman can. 120, 614, 680.

"§2. In causis in quibus tum Ecclesia tum civilis potestas aeque competentes sunt, quaeque dicuntur mixti fori, est locus praeventioni.

"Can. 1554. Actor, qui causas mixti fori ad iudicem ecclesiasticum deductas ad forum saeculare iudicandas defert, congruis poenis puniri potest ad norman can. 2222 et privatur iure contra

XIV. 23—A Consistory at St. Peter's, 1924

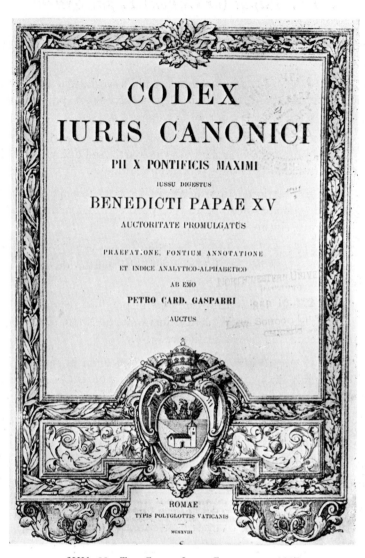

XIV. 22—The Codex Juris Canonici of 1917

[*967*]

eandem personam de eadem re et de connexis causam agendi in foro ecclesiastico. . . . .

"Can. 1742. §1. Iudex ad eruendam veritatem facti quod publice interest ut extra dubium ponatur, debet partes interrogare.

§2. In aliis casibus potest unum ex contendentibus interrogare non solum ad instantiam alterius partis, sed etiam ex officio, quoties agitur de illustranda probatione adducta.

§3. Interrogatio partium fieri a iudice potest in quovis stadio iudicii ante conclusionem in causa; post conclusionem in causa servetur praescriptum can. 1861.

"Can. 1743. §1. Iudici legitime interroganti partes respondere tenentur et fateri veritatem, nisi agatur de delicto ab ipsis commisso.

"§2. Si pars legitime interrogata respondere recuset, quanti facienda sit haec recusatio, utrum iusta sit, an confessioni aequiparanda, necne, iudicis est aestimare. . . . . .

"Can. 1744. Iusiurandum de veritate dicenda in causis criminalibus nequit iudex accusato deferre; in contentiosis, quoties bonum publicum in causa est, debet illud a partibus exigere; in aliis, potest pro sua prudentia."

There remain today a few Catholic jurists (but they are found even in America) who look back with vain longing to the palmy days of Innocent III, and maintain the medieval doctrine that the papal church's rule of conduct may prevail over the national law; that the papal church may by rights dominate the State; and that a Catholic's superior allegiance, in case of conflicting rules, may be to the church and not his country's government. The Catholic Church stands in the forefront of the Christian Churches in its theology, its logic, and its wide and wholesome moral influence. And the service rendered by the Church's legal system, in its day, was immeasurable. It is indeed difficult to imagine how Europe could have survived the civic anarchy of the Middle Ages had there been (in Barry's felicitous phrase) "no central, supreme, acknowledged power like the Papacy, guardian at once of faith, of learning, and of law". But that historic service to the law is now only history. The Consistory still meets.[23] But the time has long passed away when the people of any modern nation would endure that their national law and politics, as in the days of Pope Innocent, could be dictated by a distant alien, a supreme autocrat, framing his laws with alien advisers in secret conclave, and responsible to no one on earth but himself.

XIV. Papal (or Canon) Legal System

Sources of Illustrations

1. *Letter of Pope Clement I.* From a photograph of an original MS. of the (False) Decretals of Isidore, furnished by the Librarian of the British Museum (B. Mus. MS. 9 B XII, f. 125).

2. *Map of the Church's Jurisdiction, A. D. 1200.* From the "Catholic Encyclopedia", vol. VIII, p. 16 (New York, Robert Appleton, 1907).

3. *Palace of the Cancelleria.* From a photograph by *Alinari Bros.*, Rome.

4. *Chamber of the Sacra Romana Rota.* From a photograph taken for the author in 1923 by special permission of the Papal authorities.

5. *Penia and Coccinus, Deans of the Rota.* From old engravings by *Grentor* and *Thibout.*

6. *A Consistory in the Sistine Chapel.* From a copy of an old engraving, the artist not traceable.

7. *Decretum Gratiani.* From a photograph, furnished by special permission of the Librarian of the Vatican Library, of p. 30, MS. No. 46, dating about A. D. 1325 (Tietze's "Catalog der Illuminierten Handschriften der Rossiana").

8. *Johannes Andreae.* From a photograph, by the *Emilia Co.*, of the monument in the Civic Museum at Bologna.

9. *Pope Gregory IX Issuing the Decretals.* From a photograph by *Alinari Bros.*, Rome, of the painting by *Raphael*, in the Vatican Loggia.

10. *Decretals of Pope Gregory IX.* From a photograph, furnished by special permission of the Librarian of the Vatican Library, of p. 77, MS. No. 113, dating about A. D. 1300-1350 (Tietze's Catalog).

11. *Bull of Innocent III.* From the facsimile in *F. Steffens*, "Lateinische Paläographie", plate 88 (Trier, Schaar, 2d ed., 1909).

12. *Innocent III.* From a photograph, by *Moscione*, Rome, of the fresco-portrait in the church at Subiaco; recommended to the author as the best one, by Monsignore Mann, of the College of Beda, Rome, the foremost living authority on the Lives of the Popes.

13. *Mandate of the Holy Inquisition.* From an original proclamation printed on cloth, purchased by the author in Madrid in 1913.

14. *Galileo before the Inquisition.* From a view by the McIntosh Stereopticon Co., Chicago, of the painting by an unidentified artist; the Frick Art Reference Library of New York has not been able to identify it.

15. *Trial of Joan of Arc.* From a photograph, in the Chicago Art Institute, of the painting by *Dumond* (somewhere in the United States). There is another painting of it, by Boutet de Monvel, in the Wm. A. Clark Collection, New York.

16. *St. Ives' Statue.* From a photograph, taken for the author, of the original in the church of St. Minihy, near Tréguier, Brittany.

17. *St. Ives Attending to the Petitions of the Poor.* From a lithograph, furnished by *Francesco Fedele*, at the Italian Ministry of Fine Arts, of the painting by *P. Berettini* and *G. B. Borghese* in the Sapienza Chapel.

18. *Pilgrims at the Tomb of St. Ives.* From a photograph by *E. Hamonic*, Tréguier.

19. *A Foreign Lawyer at the Tomb of St. Ives.* From a photograph, taken in 1913, by *Frank B. Dains*, of the University of Kansas.

20. *King Louis IX Administering Justice.* From a photograph, furnished by courtesy of *Stephen S. Szlapka*, Esq., of the Paris Bar, of the fresco-painting by *Cabanel* in the Pantheon, Paris.

21. *Council of Trent.* From a photograph, furnished by *Stephen S. Szlapka*, Esq., of the Paris Bar, of the painting by *Titian* in the Louvre Museum.

22. *Codex Juris Canonici of 1917.* From the title-page of the edition of 1918, printed at the Vatican Polyglot Press.

23. *Consistory at St. Peter's, 1924.* From a photograph by the New York Times Rotograph.

Sources of Documents Quoted in Text

a. Letter of Pope Clement I. The full text reads, as given in *P. Hinschius*, "Decretales Pseudo-Isidorianae", 1863, page 53, par. LVII (furnished in copy by courtesy of the Librarian of Union Theological Seminary, New York): "Vestrum enim, qui legatione christi fungimini, est docere populos, eorum vero est vobis obedire ut deo. Si autem vobis episcopis non obedierint omnes presbiteri, diaconi ac subdiaconi et reliqui clerici cuncti, *omnesque principes* tam maioris ordinis quam et inferioris, *atque reliqui populi*, tribus et lingue non obtemperaverint, non solum infames, sed et extorres a regno dei et consortio fidelium a liminibus sanctae dei ecclesiae alieni erunt. Nam vestrum est eos instruere, *eorum vero est vobis obedire, ut deo.*"

b. Decree of Valentinian III, A. D. 445 ("Novellae Constitutiones", ed. Haenel, 1844, tit. XVI, §3, col. 175): "Hac perenni sanctione decernimus, ne quid tam episcopis gallicanis, quam aliarum provinciarum contra consuetudinem veterem liceat sine viri venerabilis papae urbis aeternae auctoritate tentare. Sed *hoc illis omnibusque pro lege sit quicquid sanxit vel sanxerit apostolicae sedis auctoritas.*"

c. Opinion of Coccinus. "Decisionum S. Rotae Romanae coram Reverendissimo Patre D. Ioanne Baptista Coccino Veneto, eiusdem Rotae olim Decano", etc., ed. DeZaulis, Pars prima, Decisio II, page 2 (Rome, Tinassius, 1672).

d. Passages from the Decretals. Translated from "Corpus Juris Canonici", ed. Friedberg, vol. II, pp. 518, 519, 746.

e. *Mandate of the Holy Inquisition:* "We the Apostolic Inquisitors against heretical depravity and apostasy in this city and archbishopric of Seville, with the Bishop of Cadiz, Ceuta, and their departments, by Apostolic authority,

"Inasmuch as, for the matters arising in the Holy Office of the Inquisition in this city and its district, there should be persons to whom the matters can be entrusted, confiding in you Sir Sebastian Hurtado of Mendoza, a native and resident of the city of Utrera, and in your diligence and care, and being informed that in your person and that of your lawful wife are found candor and the other needful virtues, and that with secrecy and loyalty, you will dispatch what may be committed to you in matters touching the Holy Office,

"By this Presents do name create and depute you as Agent of the Holy Office, to be one of those for the city of Utrera, and as such to enjoy all honors, liberties, and privileges, which according to Law, Apostolic charters, Statutes, and Decrees of this Kingdom and the procedure and directions of this office are and ought to be enjoyed by its Agents.

"And we give you license to employ throughout our District arms offensive and defensive [obscure] . . . . when engaged in the work of the Holy Office and not otherwise.

"And we require on the King's behalf and exhort on our own all Judges, Justices, and their officials in this District to treat and hold you as our Agent and to observe the said Privileges customary for such agents, and not to impede you in the use of Arms as aforesaid, and to abstain from taking jurisdiction of any criminal cases touching your person, other than offences excepted by law, remanding such cases to the competent Judges, to wit ourselves, ...

"Given at the Inquisition of Seville and Royal Castle of Triana on 5th day of January 1793".

[Signatures]

"By order of the Holy Office
Dr. Da Salvador Fortolero"

f.   *St. Ives.*   In the long list of saints, there are indeed two others who have been lawyers, but they have no general fame; see the Illinois Law Review for March, 1928 (vol. XXII, No. 7, p. 199).

There is an extensive literature about St. Ives; the following works are accessible in the Elbert H. Gary Law Library of Northwestern University: *Borderic et al.*, eds., "Monuments originaux de l'histoire de Saint Yves" (Saint Brieuc, Prudhomme, 1887; contains the depositions filed at the hearing for canonization).

A. LeGrand, "Les Vies des Saints de la Bretagne Armorique" (Quimper, Salaun, 1901).

M. S. Ropartz, "Histoire de Saint Yves" (Saint Brieuc, Prudhomme, 1856). *A. du Bois de la Villerabel*, "La Légende merveilleuse de Monseigneur Sainct Yves" (Rennes, Cailliére, 1889).

Paul Henry, "Saint Yves, avocat, justicier, ami des faibles et des petits" (Rennes, date?).

Abbé *France*, "Saint Yves: étude sur sa vie et son Temps" (Saint Brieuc, Prudhomme, 2d ed., 1892).

Emile Jobbé-Duval, "Les idées primitives dans la Bretagne contemporaine" (Paris, Sirey, 1920; originally published in the "Nouvelle revue historique de droit français et étranger", vols. 33-38).

g.   Statutes of 24 H. VIII, c. 12, 25 H. VIII, c. 19, and 26 H. VIII, c. 1 (Statutes at Large, Pickering ed., vol. 4, pp. 257, 283, 312).

h.   Lib. II, Tit. VII, cap. I, Canon 218, §1: "Romanus pontifex, Beatri Petri in privatu Successor, habet non solum primatum honoris, sed supremam et plenam potestatem jurisdictionis in universam Ecclesiam tum in rebus quae ad fidem et mores, tum in iis quae ad disciplinam et regimen Ecclesiae per totum orbem diffusae pertinent."   "The legal status of the Roman Catholic Church as a non-established church in this country was elaborately examined and defined in the case already referred to, viz.: O'Keeffe v. Cullen, which was an action by a parish priest who sought, by way of suing Cardinal Cullen for defamation, to challenge the validity of a sentence of suspension from and deprivation of the office of parish priest. The position was there laid down, and accepted ever since, as that of a voluntary association of persons who agree to accept and to be bound by certain doctrine and discipline and to submit to the authority of certain voluntary ecclesiastical tribunals, these tribunals in the case of the Catholic Church administering and applying the body of law and system of procedure of the Roman Canon Law." (Kennedy, C. J., in O'Callaghan v. O'Sullivan, Irish Reports, Free State, I, 90, 113; 1925).

i.   Codex Juris Canonici, Canons 1553, 1554, 1742-1744, as printed in Rev. *P. Chas. Augustine,* "A Commentary on the New Code of Canon Law", vol. VII, pp. 3, 186.

General References

"Corpus Juris Canonici", ed. Friedberg (Leipzig, 2 vols. 2d ed., 1879-1881).

"Codex Juris Canonici, Pii X Pontificis Maximi jussu digestus Benedicti Papae XV auctoritate promulgatus", ed. Card. Gasparri (Rome, Vatican Press, 1918).

William Barry, "The Papal Monarchy" (New York, Putnam, 1911); from this work, a masterpiece in style and judiciousness, a few sentences have been borrowed in the text above.

J. F. Schulte, "Die Geschichte der Quellen und Literatur des Canonischen Rechts" (Stuttgart, Enke, 3 vols. 1875-77).

P. Chas. Augustine, "A Commentary on the New Code of Canon Law" (St. Louis, Herder, 8 vols., 4th ed., 1921-23).

Peter A. Baart, "The Roman Court" (New York, 4th ed., 1899).

Charles Z. Lincoln, "The Civil Law and the Church" (New York, 1908).

Ethelred Taunton, "The Law of the Church: A Cyclopedia of Canon Law, etc." (London, 1906).

John A. Ryan and *M. F. Z. Millar,* "The State and the Church" (New York, 1922).

H. A. Ayrinhac, "General Legislation in the New Code of Canon Law", and other volumes (New York, Benziger, 1920+).

S. Woywod, "A Practical Commentary on the Code of Canon Law" (New York, 2 vols., 2d ed. 1926).

[*974*]

Sources

P. Hinschius, "System des Katholischen Kirchenrechts mit besonderer Rücksicht auf Deutschland" (Berlin, 6 vols., 1869-1897).

G. O. Nations, "The Canon Law of the Papal Throne" (New York, 1926).

E. J. Tardif, "Histoire des sources du droit canonique" (Paris, 1887).

Carlo Calisse, "Diritto ecclesiastico" (Florence, 1902).

F. Egon Schneider, "Die Römische Rota, nach geltendem Rechte auf geschichtlicher Grundlage", Band I (Paderborn, 1914).

Harold D. Hazeltine, "Roman and Canon Law in the Middle Ages" (chap. XXI of vol. V, "Cambridge Medieval History", 1926).

Frederic W. Maitland, "Roman Canon Law in the Church of England" (London, 1898).

Arthur Ogle, "The Canon Law in Medieval England" (London, 1912).

Continental Legal History Series (Boston, Little, Brown & Co.):

Vol. I: *J. Brissaud*, "General Survey, etc." part IX (1912).

Vol. VII: *Engelmann-Millar*, "History of Continental Civil Procedure" (1927).

Vol. V: *A. Esmein*, "History of Continental Criminal Procedure" (1913).

Vol. IX: *J. Brissaud*, "History of French Public Law" (1915).

XV
The Romanesque Legal System

(*I*)   *Resurrection of Justinian's Law-Books*

1. Bologna and the Germanic conquerors.

2. Irnerius' lectures—Justinian's texts.

3. The first law school—Government by students—
   Records of the law-student guilds.

4. Eminent status of the law-professor—The glossators.

(*II*)   *Adaptation of Roman Law*

5. The practicians—Opinions on cases—Bartolus.

6. New court-houses in Italy and France—Palais de
   Justice at Paris.

7. Spread of Roman law studies—Bracton and Azzo.

8. Shift of leadership from Italy—Cujas in France.

9. Netherlands and Scotland.

10. Germany—Reception of Roman Law—Carpzov—
    Windscheid and Von Ihering.

(*III*)   *Nationalization of Roman Law*

11. Roman law as a secondary law only, alongside of
    local law.

12. The nationalizers, Dumoulin, Colbert, Pothier, in
    France.

13. Code Napoleon—Nationalization in other countries.

(*IV*)   *Expansion of Romanesque Law*

14. Scientific and political motives—Spread of Roman-
    esque law to other continents.

THE
ROMANESQUE
LEGAL SYSTEM

XV
The Romanesque Legal System

(I) First Period

FOR five centuries the Roman empire had been a ruin, and Justinian's law-books had long been unknown or unstudied. Suddenly in the 1100's, the city of Bologna[1] became the center of one of the greatest intellectual phenomena recorded in European history,—the resurrection of Justinian's law-texts. Those resurrected books were destined once more to impress the Roman legal system not only on Europe but far beyond it.

Panorama di Bologna.

XV. 1—Bologna
This city became the center of the revival of the Roman texts

[*981*]

XV. Romanesque Legal System

Bologna was now one of a hundred city-states in Italy in which a new civic life was building up after the settlement of the Germanic conquerors in their new lands. The general conditions of armed self-help, typical of those days, are revealed in the tall square fighting towers, each the fortress of a powerful family, a Capulet or a Montague. Some are still standing today; they were once the common feature of all Italian medieval cities.[2] After the gradual collapse of Roman rule, about A. D. 500, and its replacement by the rule of Goths, Franks, and Lombards, the conquered peoples of Italy, Gaul, and Spain had been left to live according to their own Romanized customs. But Roman legal science had been buried, apparently forever. Even in such centres of old Roman life as Bologna and the

XV. 2—THE FEUDAL FIGHTING TOWERS OF MEDIEVAL PAVIA

XV. 3—Irnerius, the Law Professor at Bologna

The teacher who popularized at Bologna the study of the resurrected
Roman law-texts. This fresco adorns the ceiling
of the Town-hall of Bologna

rest of Northern Italy, the new hordes of alien conquerors were slow in developing. The very rudiments of knowledge were confined to the monks and clergy. All relics of classic pagan learning were despised by the early Christian converts. The hundreds of petty domains were ruled by force, hardly by law. Systematic justice had been shattered, and was growing again slowly and in court practice only. There were no schools nor teachers of law. In short, jurisprudence, the one science of the Romans, had gone, and the Germanics had brought nothing fit to take its place.

2. Amid these conditions, about A. D. 1100, the name of Irnerius appears, as the symbol of a new learning,—the "bright lamp of law", he was called.[3] We know less about Irnerius' personality than we do about Gaius or about Shakespeare; yet it must have been one of the great inspiring personalities of the ages. The period was one of general intellectual revival in North Italy. But historians have not yet fully explained just why its most remarkable feature should have been a concentration on legal science, and just why that concentration should take the form of this wondrous resurrection of Justinian's law-books,—virtually lost and buried for five centuries past. This much is certain, that a young genius named Irnerius, about A. D. 1100, was revered by his successors as the founder of the

XV. 4—JUSTINIAN'S DIGEST
This is page 1 of the unique manuscript at Florence

new learning, and that he began to lecture on Justinian's Code and Digest. These texts[4] he exalted as embodying pure legal science, "written reason", far above the crude customs and court practice around him.

He proved to be the man of the hour. His enthusiasm and eloquence had the inspiration of a crusade. Within another century, there were said to be ten thousand students, chiefly in law, at Bologna, crowding thither from all over Europe. They now formed a "studium generale", or university,—the first Christian one in Europe, earlier even than those of Paris and Oxford.

In the great square of San Stefano[5] the traveler may still see the place at which Irnerius is said to have held forth; for in those days the masters lectured in their own houses, or in rented rooms, but if the class of a popular master was large, he lectured in the open air in a public place.

The earliest law diploma extant dates from A. D. 1276. Its language is less concise and more intimate than the forms of today:[a]

". . . . . . . Assiduous toil, daily zeal, and prolonged devotion to the study of civic science, merit a reward, so that toil may be transformed into rest, study into profit, and long devotion into perpetual satisfaction. It is therefore fitting that we grant the rewards of virtue to those that merit them and solace the studious with the fruits of toil. Hence the wise, upright, provident, and sage

Bologna
Chiesa S. Stefano e Palazzo Isolani

XV. 5—THE SQUARE OF SAN STEFANO, AT BOLOGNA
In this square Irnerius is said to have held forth to
his throngs of law students

Doctor Peter Amadeo Kiginkola of Brescia, having auspiciously completed his study of the Civil Law, has aspired to receive our sanction, and inasmuch as he has been found most sufficient, as we have been informed by the learned men, to wit [naming the Faculty of Law] . . . we now in the presence of the said Doctors and Scholars do grant him the license here and everywhere to teach the Civil Law and to hold a master's chair. .

"Done at Reggio," etc., etc.

3. But although the masters were the ones who conferred this diploma of admission to their guild, they were not then, as they are today, the rulers of the University. Bologna was a students' university,—a type all its own. The professor[6] was, as it were, a learned adventurer, own-

XV. 6—A Law Lecturer and His Class

ing some precious manuscripts containing valuable knowledge, and employed by a number of independent gentlemen—the students—to teach them the secrets of that knowledge.   The students hired, paid, and discharged the professors; and they took active measures to secure the full value of their fees.   They bound the professor by strict rules and penalties; he was fined if he began one minute after the church bell rang at seven in the morning; he was fined if he continued one minute after the bell rang at nine; he was fined if he skipped a chapter of text of Justinian, or if he evaded a difficult passage.   He must not dawdle or meander; for the whole text of Justinian was divided into numbered points, and the professor was fined if he did not reach each point by a given date. Moreover, he deposited a sum of money in advance with a banker, and his fines were deducted by the banker on order of the student committee.

The whole student-body was divided into guilds (or fraternities), called "nations".   These nations were well organized, held meetings, and kept elaborate records, some of them very handsomely illuminated.[7, 8] Each nation, or guild, included the men from a particular region, —English, German, Hungarian, Bohemian, Gascon, and so on; in Bologna there came to be fourteen foreign nations

XV. 7—THE BOLOGNA STUDENT RECORDS

This is the title-page of a volume of the Law Nation's
records of A. D. 1502

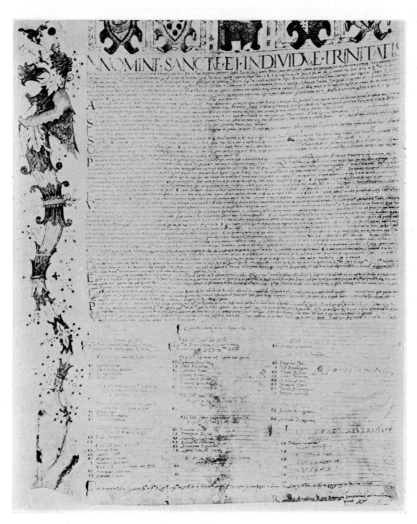

XV. 8—A Page from the Bologna Law-Student Records

and four Italian nations.　These student-chronicles teem with candid narratives of armed quarrels with the other student nations, and of lively disputes over the appointment and pay of the professors.　For example, opening at random the records of the captain of the German law nation at Padua, we read:[b]

"On Nov. 15 Cyriac Adler of Gratz was taken to jail.　The reason was this: In this country it is a great privilege to carry arms, but you must have a license.　All sorts of persons manage to get the license, by various expedients, but usually on the pretext of being some sort of an officer.　Cyriac went and got a license all right, but somehow or other he was given away, and the police arrested him. I called a meeting of the German nation at the shop of John the barber next morning early, to take action.　We decided to ask Dr. Marco Blanco, professor of criminal law, to help us, as he is a very good friend of our nation".

And so, the captain's record tells us, finally they got Cyriac released on bonds.

Each nation of students elected annually its captain, or rector; and the captain was entitled, at the close of his office, to affix on the walls of the court-yard and the lecture halls his family escutcheon, in colors.　In the University of Padua, three thousand of these escutcheons may still be seen preserved, completely filling the walls of the central cloister above and below and also of the Great Lecture Hall; in this Hall, Galileo taught mathematics for ten years.[9]

[*990*]

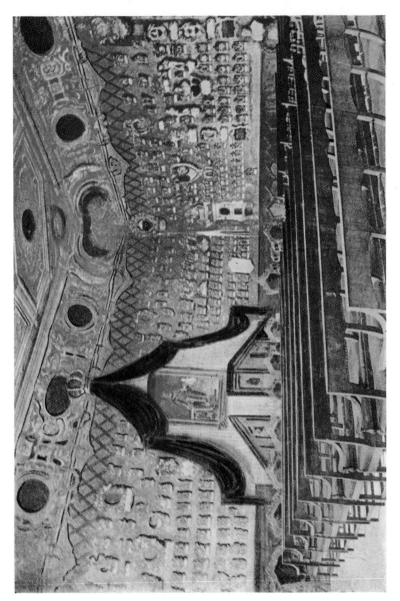

XV. 9—Escutcheons of Nation-Captains

Some three thousand of these may still be seen on the walls of the University at Padua

3. Law Studies at Bologna

New universities, mainly of law students, soon sprang up in Northern Italy,—a dozen of them; and new masters arose, whose fame went over Europe. Popes and Emperors granted charters of privilege to the Universities. The title of "Doctor" now signified an order of intellectual nobility. How preëminent was their status is shown by the monumental tombs[10] of the professors of law, erected to their honor in the public places of the cities; the stone casket was placed within the upper tier of columns. This peculiar architectural style is still a feature of Bologna and Padua.

Bologna

4. In this great movement Irnerius' role was to exalt the pure science of the newly resurrected Roman texts. He and his immediate successors, known as glossators, descanted on these texts with glosses, or explanations. When later these were printed, they took the form of solid marginal blocks of print around a

XV. 10—Tomb of a Jurist at Bologna

a pilato
res legum fu
erut pagani.

I N nomine domini.Hoc in compilatione Dige
ſtorum fuit dictum,nō quando leges ſactę fuerunt
qa pagani erant:vt.C.de vete.iure enu.l.j.ſic et alś
facit inſti. in procœ.in prin.

b   Perpetui.id eſt generalis.

c   Auguſti. Quia
ſemper huius appoſi
ti debet eſſe , vt au
geat imperiū , licet
non ſemper augeat.
ſic et matrimonium
indiuidua cōiunctio
dicitur:tamē diuidi
tur quádoqʒ: vt. C.
de repud. l. cōſenſu.
ſed propoſitum con
ſideratur:vt inſti.de
pa.poæin prin.

† In vetuſtis
exemplari -
bus deſunt
hęc verba,in
nomine do-
mini amen.
† non eſt, p-
petui Augu-
ſti.vel dicɩ p
petuo ɩ ſem-
per Auguſti,
hɩc ſomniat,
generalis.

d   Enucleati. p ſi
militudinem vocat
ius enucleatū, ʒ no
bis eſt traditum in li
bris Pandectarū. Si
cut enim antequā p-
ueniatur ad nucleū
interiorē nucis: vnū
amariſsimū,et aliud
durum,et aliud ama
rū,& quarto ad nu
cleum dulcē perueni
tur:ita & in multitu
dine antiquorum li
brorum amaritudi-
nes inueniuntur.i.di
ſcordiæ infinitæ.itē
duritię.i.iniquæ ſen
tentię,et aliæ nō ſic
iniquæ,in quibuſdā tū locis quædā latebant dulcedines.i. æ-
quiſsimæ ſententiæ,velut lilia inter ſpinas:& illas dulces ſen
tentias Iuſtinianus ex alɩjs excerpſit,& nobis tradidit legen-
das:vnde ipſe,dicitur tradere ius enucleatum.ſecundum Io.

* Intellige,
per adopio-ti
nem: quia re
vera nepos
eius ex ſoro-
re fuit. Egɩ.
per.

e   Collecti.ex his.i.ex eo quod dixit in princi.pōt colligi qs
fuerit autor ſiue cōpilator:qa Iuſtinianus filius Iuſtini *,vt in
ſit.de dona.ʃ.eſt & aliud.Item quæ materia.i.oia vetera iura
antiquorum prudentium.quæ intentio.i.vt colligas ius enucleatū in vnum volumē.V tɩ̓litas per ſe patet:et qa citius adipiſci poteſt ʒ
olim.Cui parti philoſophię ſupponatur: & quidem Ethicæ,
qa de moribus tractat hoc volumen,ſicut alia duo volumina.

IN NOMINE

Domini [a] † Amen.Iuſti
niani ſacratiſsimi principis p-
petui[b] Auguſti[c] † iuris enu
cleati[d] ex omniuetere iure col
lecti [e] Digeſtorum,ſeu Pan
dectarum Liber primus.

TITVLVS   I.

DE IVSTITIA
ET IVRE.

Vlpianus lib.j.Inſtitutionum.   I.

Vri ſ o
perā da
turum
prius[g]
noſſe o
portet ,
vnde no
men iuris deſcendat. Eſt au
tem ius à iuſtitia [h] appella

XV. 11—TEXT OF JUSTINIAN'S DIGEST WITH GLOSS
The text here shown is the beginning of Book I

o ¶ Sim̄ꝗ̉ dinez. nam ibi scīpit nō fieri signa. vt.ſ. de veteri ſpe.c.l.ij. §. hoc aūt.

b ¶ Et ꝺigeſtoꝛ. vt.ſ. ꝺe ve.iur.e.l.ij. hoc aūt.

c ¶ Ampliorem. ſ. chartaꝛ.

¶ De ſumma trinitate ꝺe iuſticia tractaturus ꝺe eius parte ſcīpua quidez
tractat id eſt reli-
gione. Religiōis
aūt eſt pncipiū fi-
des: ꬁ hanc pōnit
nr. vel ſic pōt cō-
tinuari. Quiā oīa
ab iſa trinitate, p
cedant vt ꝺicīur
in euāgelio Ioā-
nis. In pncipio
erat verbuz ꭛c. ꭛
ſ. ꝺe ve.iu.e.l.ſ.
circa pncī. mer-
to igī ꝺe ſumma
trinitate ꭛ fide ca
tbolica ꭛ca ſup-
ponit̄. ꭛ hec cōn-
tinuatiō tangit pri
mā tr꭛ prez Rcc.
Vel ſic cōnua:
et tangit ſcꝺa pa
buꝰ Rcc. quiā
omne ꝗ̉ nō eſt
er fide ſit peccatū
vt extra ꝺe pſeri.
qᷓ omne. xxviij
q.ſ.c ꭛ infᷓ re-
paratio a fide ſu-
pllit exodiū. ꭛ nul
boni poſſit ſine fi
ꝺe ſuperedificari
vbi fides ꝺeſt fun-
damentū. vt.ſ. q.
j. cū pauls. Ideo
imꝑatoꝛ Iuſtini-
anus ſui opio po-
ſuit ſummā trini-
tatem ꭛ fidem ca
tbolicam funda-
mentum.

scribi iuſſimus: vt omne ꝗ̉ a
nobis compoſituz eſt hic ꭛ in
ſcriptura: ꭛ in iſa ſanctōe pu-
rum atꝗ dilucidū clareat. licet ex hac cauſa in ampliozem
numerū ſumma huiꝰ codicis
redacta eſt. ¶ Vt igī ſanctiſ
ſimi ꭛ flozentiſſimi patres no
ſtri labozeovobis manifeſti fi
ant: ꭛ p omne tempus obtine
ant. hanc pntez legē ad freꝗn
tiſſimū ordinē veſtrū ꝺuriꝰ
uſtinandū.

Incipit liber primus Iuſti
mianꝰ ꝺe ſumma trinitate et
fide catholica vt nemo publice ꝺe ea contendere aude
at. Rubrica.   Titulꝰ.ſ.

p ¶ Inſinuata.i.docta.   q ¶ Damaſum. papam.

r ¶ Apoſtolice. ex hoc ꝗ hic legitur ſume.ar. ꝗ vſure hō
die peti non poſſint ſm ius ciuile. nam ꝺicit imperator ꝗ
vult ꝗ ſubdin ſibi ſequantur fidem ſiue religionem quam
Petrus apoſtolus tradidit romanis. ſed iure ꝺiuino pro
hibite ſunt vſure,
ergo peti non poſ-
ſunt vſure Ite iu-
ra ciuila nō ꝺeci-
gnantur ſacros ca
nones imitari: vt
aūt.ꝺe ec.n. Vn-
ꝺe ꝺomini? Az. in
ſumma ꝺe vſuris
conceſſit ꝗ ſ꭛꭛ nō
poſſet peti. verum
tamen c aſſīgn le-
gem poſſ꭛ rideri
ꝗ ꝺicit ſequi ꝗtuz
ad fide. ad hoc ri-
ꝺent quidā ita: ꝗ
ſacre leges non ꝺi
cūt ꝗ ſint pꝛohi-
bite ne capiāt vſu
re in quatnoꝛ con-
ciiis. ſed quidam
ꝺecreuiſte ꝺicūt ꝗ
ſunt pꝛohibite: ſed
diſtingue aut pe-
tuntur vt lucrum
ant quia abſit ſibi
quia paſſus eſt ꝺā
num ꭛ tunc nō vt
vſure ſed intereſſe
petunt.ar.ff.ꝺ pꝛo-
cio.l. ſocius qui in
eo. ꭛ ita obſeruaſ i
curia romana.

¶ Appꝛo Gratianus et Va-
lentinianus et Theodoſius
aaa. ad populam vrbis con-
ſtantinopolitane.

Vnctos
populos
ꝗs ꞇcle-
métie no
ſtre regit
impiū in
tali volu
mine reli-
gione verſari: quaz ꝺiuinum
Petrum apoſtolus tradidiſ-
ſe romanis religio vſꝗ ad-
huc ab iſo inſinuata ꝺecla-
rat. quāꝗ pontifice Dama
ſuz ſequi claret. ꭛ Petrū alexā
ꝺrie epiſcopū virū apoſtolice
ſanctitatis. hoc eſt vt ſm apo
ſtolicam diſciplinā ꭛ euange
licamꝗ ꝺoctrinā patris et fi
lij et ſpūſancti vnam Trinitatem ſub pari maieſtate ꭛ ſub
pia trinitate credamus. hāc
legem ſequentes chriſtiano-
rum catholicorum nomen iu
bemus amplecti. reliquos ve
ro ꝺementes veſanoſꝗ iudi-
cantes heretici ꝺogmatis in-
famiā ſuſtinere ꝺiuina pmuz

a ¶ Sanctitatis.
non ꝺicit ideo ꝗ
fuerit apoſtolꝰ. nā
tr꭛ vnum Petrū
leginius apoſto-
lum fuiſſe. ſed vi-
tam egit apoſtoli-
cam.

e ¶ Fide. fides eſt ſperandarum rerum credulitas ꭛ non
tamen cuiuſlibet rei ſed circa trinitatem. ꭛ argumentum
non apparentium.

f ¶ Catholica.id e vniuerſali ꭛ vbiꝗ porrecta. vnde ꝺia
turʒ in omnem terram exiuit ſonus eoꝛ.

g ¶ Contendere. aliꝰ eſt tractare.i. ꝺiſputare. ꭛c.

¶ Cunctos. pmᷓ pars ſcīpit fidem ſeru. aʒ quā ſancti pa
tres tradiderūt. Scꝺo alliei pmᷓ ſeruātes. Tercio affi-
cit pena triplici nō ſeruantes. ꭛c.

b ¶ Quos.ar. ꝗ ſi Bononienſis cōuenᷓ Mutine nō
ꝺeberi iudicari ſm ſtatuta mutine quibꝰ nō ſubeſt quia
ꝺicat quos noſtre clemencie.

i ¶ Clemencie. clemēcia eſt pars moꝺeſtie. moꝺeſtia eni
cōuenit ſuperiorib9 ꭛ inferiorib9. ſed pꝛopie eſt a ſuperio-
ribus erga inferiores exercere clemenciam: vt.j.ſam̄. her
aſ.ſ.in ipſius.

k ¶ Religione.id eſt fide.

l ¶ Qua꭛.id eſt qualem ꭛ ꝺic ꝗ religio eſt ius cuiuſdam
ſuperiore nature que curā ceremoniáꝗ nobis affert.
Item et eo ꝗ̉ ꝺicit volumuns. ergo eſt lex. vt inſti. ꝺe iur.
n.ſ. ſed ꝗ pncipi. ꭛c.

m ¶ Religio. circa fidem.

f ¶ Scꝺm applicam. quia apoſtoli ita pꝺicauerunt.

v ¶ Euangelica. ita continet in euangelio.

z ¶ Hanc. ecce pmuſ ꝗ ſeruus vocat noſe ꝺni.

y ¶ Reliquos. terciu ꝺeinde. ꭛c.

z ¶ Dementes. id eſt ſine mente.

a ¶ Infamiam. ecce vna pena et collige hic ar. ꝗ periu
rius puniendus ſit. licet.ſ.ꝺe re.cre. et ꝺe iureiuran.l.ij.ꝺi-
catur ꝗ non ꝺebeat punir corporaliter. punitur tame alis
vt hic. leges enim que periuria puniunt ꭛c. vt.ſ.ꝺe indi
cta fidu.l.penul.

b ¶ Suſtinere. iubemus.

c ¶ Diuina. ſcꝛ eccleſiaſtica quia ſepant a cōmunione fide
liuri ꭛ ꝗ ꝺicat eos infames ergo nō pñt ferre teſtimonius:
vt.ff.ꝺe teſti.l.iij. §. legis iul. ꝺe vi. ꝗ lex inter eos ꭛ in con
tractibus ꭛ in teſtamētis ꭛ inter alios cōcedit: vt.ſ.ꝺe here
ti.l.qᷓ.in part. ꭛ in fi. Sol. hic loquiʒ ꝺe infamia facti: que
non repellit a teſtimonio ꝺe qua loquiʒ: ꭛ ff. ꝺe obſequi ſ
l.ij. vel aliʒ hic loquiʒ ꝺe infamia iuris ſed loquiʒ ꝺe iis ꭛
reiieiis qui nunꝗ teſtificari pñt: qui ꭛ in illa lege aſſignᷓ ꭛
vel tercio repellit eos teſtim inter onthodozos. ſed inter ſe
non excepti quibuſdam. quia etiam inter ſe repelluñt: vt
in illa lege qñ. vel ꝺic eos infames non iſo iure ſed ꝛ pſen-

---

XV. 12—JUSTINIAN'S CODE, PRINTED WITH THE GLOSS
This is from the edition of A. D. 1488, one of the earliest

[993]

central core of text.[11]   Each master added to these glosses.
The texts of Justinian were now multiplied by hand-copies
on parchment, and spread all over Western Europe; even
in England, Bracton in A. D. 1250 had a copy as he wrote
"De Legibus Angliae".   And when the great art of book-
printing arrived, in the late 1400's, the gloss style was still
used; and one of the most popular books, other than theological, was Justinian's Corpus Juris; one of the first
complete editions of the Corpus Juris was that printed by
Koberger, at Nuremberg, in A. D. 1488, in the gloss style.[12]

(II) SECOND PERIOD

5.   Up to this time the Justinian books had been
studied as pure science, much as Kant's Philosophy or
Mill's Logic might be studied today.   But after two centuries of this, a new type of jurist arose, destined to apply
this pure science to the legal practice of the day.   These
men were known as Practicians, or Commentators.   They
gave opinions on law-cases and wrote independent treatises.

These commentaries were in style a marked advance
on the glosses or marginal notes.   These men now for the
first time applied the ancient principles of the Roman
texts to the Germanic and feudal customs.   Roman law
began to be transformed into Italian law.   The practical
spirit of these Commentators may be illustrated by a page[13]

Aec figura differt à præce.nam hic ripa continetur tribus lineis.f.a.b.&,b.c.&, c. d. & habet duos angulos.f.in puncto.b.& in puncto.c.tota igitur hæc alluuio debet diuidi iure propinquitatis, quæ tota continetur infra plura latera. Primo igitur ducatur linea rubea per medium super angulum b.& fit linea b.e.deinde ducatur linea per medium diuidens super angulum c. & erit linea e. f. quæ duæ lineæ fecabunt se in puncto g.dico ergo quod portio alluuionis pertinens ad agrum Titij in dicto puncto g. fiunatur: quia fi eft azurea fuper puncto.g. vtráque lineam

punctualiter tangeret ergo ille eft punctus,in quo vtriufque propinquitas termi-atur. Si vero excederes,& velics facere circulum fupra punctum e.& fe vni partium accederet: & ab alia elongaretur quod auc eft intra illud triangulū b.g.e. per tinet ad præ-dum Titij iure propinquitatis:quod patet: quia infra illum triangulum panditur per cētrum vnius circuli in puncto h qui tangat punctualiter ripam Titij, nullam aliam ripā tangit inter Luciū & Caiū per lineā directō ductā víq; ad flumen.& hæc fufficiant de ripa quæ habet lineā vel lineas rectas. Restat videre de ripa quæ habet lineā circularem &c.

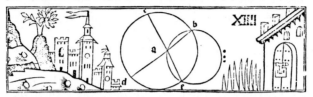

D euidentiam eorum quæ dicenda funt de figura circulari, fciendum eft, quòd circulus eft figura plana,vna quidem linea contenta, quæ circunfe-rentia nominatur in cuius medio punctus eft à quo omnes lineæ ad circunferentiam exiftentes funt fibi-vnicem æquales, vt dicit Euclides in prima figura. Nam cen-trum eft in puncto a. & omnes in lineæ inde exiftentes funt fibi vnicem æquales, & fi plures dicerentur idem effet. Item apparet quòd omnes lineæ prædictæque circunferentia in centrum faciunt angulum. Item præmitto quòd totum illud quod eft in circulo infra aliquas lineas duas eft magis propinquum illi parti circunferentiæ quæ in punctis duar-

rū linearū terminatur.vt verbi gratia affumas parte circunfe-rentiæ b.c.& duæ lineam rectam ad centrum. & facit triangu-lum b.a.c.& dico quod quicquid eft infra illum triangulum eft magis propinquum illi parti circunferentiæ b.c.quam ali cui alij quod patet ad fenium, & poteft probari. Nam pona-tur centrum in aliqua parte infra dictum triangulū. & fupra illum ducatur circulus azureus, qui tangit punctualiter di-ctam partem b.c.dico quod nullam aliam partem circunfe-rentiæ tangeret: ergo illi magis propinquā: & idem dicendū eft de eo qui continetur infra illum triangulum b.a.d.& infra illum triangulum a.b.d. & a.e.d. & fupra illum triangulum c.a.e.vt euidenter apparet &c.

Via in præcedenti dictum eft, quòd lineæ funt du-ctæ á centro ad circunferentiam,& quandoque ignoratur, vbi fit centrum. Et ideo expedit quòd ducatur linea a circunferentia verius centrum, vel quòd á centrum f. ueniatur : ideo facta eft hæc figura quæ duos h.bc.at circulo,& fic hoc fieri docet duobus modis. Primo fic,fit ce-ntrum, quod apponatur in circunferentia vnus pun-ctus.b. & ab vtraque parte eiufdem puncti,duo alij æque di-ftantes c.d.deinde ducatur linea recta.c.d.& iftius linea inue-niat medium in puncto.e.deinde ducatur linea recta.b.e.di-co quòd de neceffitate,ifta vadit directē fupra centrum,fcili-cet punctum.a. vt probatur in princi.lib. Eucli. hoc etiam patet:quia idem in alia parte circunferentiæ ponatur pun-ctus. f. & ab vtraque parte duo puncti æque diftantes. g. h. deinde inueniatur medium dictæ lineæ in puncto i. deinde ducatur linea recta f.i.dico quod ifta de neceffitate vaditver-fus centrum,& fi vltra pretendatur linea.b.e.& linea f.i.fecabunt fe ta puncto a. vt erit centrum Concluditur ergo q̄ ibi, vbi dictæ lineæ fe fecant,de neceffitate eft centrum. hoc etiam fieri alio modo ad idem tendenti, docet fecundus cir-culus. Ponitur enim quòd fit circulus centrum aut non vi-

detur in puncto a.ponatur in circunferentia punctus b.& ab vtraque parte eiufdem puncti,duo alij æque diftantes c.d.de inde ponatur pes circini in puncto.d.& extendatur víque ad punctum.e.& voluatur fupra,& infra circulum. eodem mo do ponatur pes circini in puncto d.& extendatur víq; ad pū ctum c.& fic illæ duæ lineæ circulares ductæ,fe fecabunt ex-tra circulum & & ita in puncto f. deinde ducatur linea c.f. dico q̄ illa de neceffitate vadit verius centrum,& eodem mo do fi in alia parte circuli idem hat,vt ponat in circunferentia punctus g. & ab vtraq; parte duo puncti æque diftantes h.i. deinde voluatur centrū fupra h.& fupra i.vt in præcedēti di ctū eft:& fic dictæ lineæ fe fecabūt in puncto k.& in puncto m.ducatur ergo linea k.m.recta : tunc illa duret ad centrū.& fic in illo puncto vbi fecabunt fe linea c.f.& linea k.m. ibi erit centrum. His præmiffis ad euidentiam dico, q̄ ripa prædio-rum quæ habet lineam circularem,quandoq; habet fe vt eo-tinentiam intra circulum,quandoq; vt extra,& eodem mo do fi vltra protendatur linea.b.e.& linea f.i.fecabunt fe vt vel cotentiā g̃ alluuio cōtinet circularē ripā,tū primo modo,ti ant ripa continens lineam circularē contine minus femicir-culo,totū autem circuli continere non pōt,quia fic flumē n̄ haberet exitum. & hæc in figuris proximis declarabunt &c.

XV. 13—BARTOLUS' TREATISE ON ALLUVION

of Bartolus on the doctrine of Alluvion,—title to land acquired by operation of water-flow; he presents several careful diagrams to show the application of the principle in different cases. The contrast with the crude Germanic Mirror of Saxony, of almost the same period, is notable.

These jurists, besides lecturing in the law schools, had a large and lucrative practice in giving opinions. Their peculiar status can best be understood from the story of Shakespeare's Portia; Portia is called into court by the party to give an opinion, which is taken as the ground of decision by the judge, and yet the jurist receives a fee from the party. Searching for a brief illustration of these opinions, one comes upon Bartolus' opinion on the wine-selling statute;[14] which seems to reveal that clients were as ingenious then as now in evading a sumptuary law:[c]

"A city statute provided that no one should sell wine at retail, under a penalty. But a certain dealer used to sell to a customer a cask or two casks or a barrel of wine, and so on to other customers, and then the buyers took delivery in flasks and jugs of various sizes. The question is whether the seller has incurred the penalty. As to this, it must be understood that some measures and weights in common use are termed gross or large, others are termed retail or small; see the law of measures; . . . . . . and those measures have to be inspected by the custom of the city; see the law of sales. . . . . Now in the said laws a barrel is gross measure, while bottles, flasks, etc., are termed retail measure. Hence, a person selling by the barrel is not selling at

[*996*]

retail. And the fact that this party measured it out to his customers in retail quantities is immaterial; for the statute speaks only of the sale.

"So say and advise

"İ, Bartolo of Sassoferrato, doctor of both laws, and have signed in testimony thereof and affixed my seal".

The most famous exponent of this applied Roman law was Bartolus,[15] about A. D. 1350, whose works dominated for two centuries or more. He was called "the monarch of the law". The saying ran, "Nemo jurista nisi Bartolista". So extraordinary was the respect paid to this jurist that the Emperor Charles IV, when ennobling him, conferred on him by charter this singular privilege, that he, and all his descendants who might be professors of law, should have the power to legitimize any bastard students who might attend their classes! So distinctive was this man's impress on the practice of law that in some schools the very program of a law lecture was described as consisting

CONSILIVM XII.

Tatutum eſt in ci-
uitate' ꝗ nullus vēdat vinum ad
minutum ſub certa pœna. modò
quidam vendidit cuidam vnam ſalmam vi
ni, aliȷ duas, aliȷ vnum barile, & ſic fecit plu
ribus: iſti emptores acceperunt vinum cùm
diuerſis flaſchis, & vaſis diuerſarum men-
ſurarum. † Quæritur an venditor in pœnā
inciderit. Circa qđ ſciendū eſt ꝗ quędā mē
ſuræ & pondera, quibus vtuntur ſunt groſ
ſæ, & magnæ: quę.dā minutę & paruæ: vt l.
modiȷs. de ſuſcepto. & arca. lib xȷ. ſic & mo
netę: vt l. numis. de leg. iiȷ. & iſtæ ſecundùm
cōſuetudinē ciuitatis debēt inſpici: vt l. Imperator. ff. de contrahen. emptio. Nūc ad p-
poſitum, menſura' groſſa eſt barile, minutæ
ſunt pittere, & focliecię, & ſimilia. † Qui er
go vendidit ad barile non vendidit ad minutum. & ſi dicatur quòd eſt menſura-
tum ad minutū, non obſtat: quia ſtatutum
loquiť de vēditione. Et ita dico & conſulo
ego Barto. à Saxofer. vtriuſꝗ iuris doctor.

XV. 14—Bartolus' Opinion on the Wine-Sale Statute

BARTOLVS DE SAXO FERRATO

Jura doces populos æqua libranda bilance
Intricata tuis, Bartole, temporibus Bh.

XV. 15—BARTOLUS

5. The Practicians

FERRARA – Palazzo di Giustizia

XV. 16—PALACE OF JUSTICE AT FERRARA, A. D. 1321

of three parts, "textus, glossa, et Bartolus",—as if an Anglican law school curriculum should be summarized by saying "common law, equity, and Chitty".

6. Bartolus and the Practicians had now carried the resurrected Roman law into the courts. A learned profession arose and multiplied. And from this period the new movement is reflected in architecture. As once in old Rome, special buildings and spacious halls were now devoted to "palaces of justice",—as they were called in Italy and France.

The court-house at Ferrara[16] is probably the third oldest extant in Europe, built A. D. 1321; only West-

[*999*]

minster and Paris are earlier. At Padua[17] may still be seen a courtroom of A. D. 1420, probably the largest courtroom in the world, larger even than Westminster Hall; it is three hundred feet long, one hundred wide, and eighty high. And there is still shown the stone-pillory in the corner of the hall, on which bankrupt debtors were exposed to the jeers of the populace in penalty for their fraud.

At Rouen, on the Seine, the capital of Normandy, still stands the superb court-house, now termed Palace of Justice,[18] started in the 1400's, one of the finest surviving monuments of Gothic art in a civic edifice. Next to Fer-

XV. 17—PALACE OF JUSTICE AT PADUA
This is the largest courtroom in the world

[*1000*]

XV. 18—PALACE OF JUSTICE AT ROUEN
The exterior court-yard and the trial courtroom

XV. 19—PALACE OF JUSTICE AT PARIS

rara and Paris, this is probably the oldest surviving court-house in Europe continuously used to the present time for that purpose; for Westminster Hall in London, though older, has now been abandoned as a courtroom.

But the most famous of these edifices is the Palace of Justice in Paris. For two thousand years, since Caesar's day, when a Roman praetor here set up his court, a temple of Law and Justice has stood on this spot.[19] Louis IX, Saint Louis, whose name is linked with justice in French tradition, here heard causes of the suitors in person, and in the 1200's here in his palace established the first court

6. *Palaces of Justice*

of appeal, or "curia regis"; later, in the 1400's, his palace was given over to the exclusive use of the Law Courts of Paris, and was thenceforth known as the Palace of Justice. One-half of the drama of French history has been enacted within these walls. In this building cluster for centuries the traditions of the French Bar, both convivial and intellectual. Here were held the revels and theatricals of the barristers' order, like the celebrated revels of the London Inns of Court. Here in the Great Room, or Gilded Room,[20] the kings of France held their beds of justice—that is, the most solemn sessions of the Supreme

XV. 20—A Session of the Supreme Court at Paris

[*1003*]

XV. 21—The Tribunal of the Terror

Court. Here in April, 1654, the young Louis XIV in boots and spurs uttered his famous words, "The State—that is Myself". Here in 1794 sat the Revolutionary Tribunal of the Terror,[21] which sent two thousand condemned persons to the guillotine in two months. And here, in the spacious Salle des Pas Perdus (or Hall of Wasted Time), long generations of French lawyers have rendezvoused with their throngs of clients in preparation for their trials.[22] The glorious record of the French Bar for professional independence and courage is equalled by none other in the world, except the Anglican. Four times in French legal history has the entire Bar resigned its functions, and left the courts without lawyers, rather than submit to the arbitrary dictation of princes and politicians. And when the Advocate-General Servin, protesting on behalf of the Supreme Court of Paris against an unjust decree, fell dead in the presence of Cardinal Richelieu and King Louis

[*1004*]

Imp. lithog. de F. Delpech

Juvenel des Ursins Chancelier de France
(Regne de Louis XI 1470.)

XV. 22a—A CHANCELLOR OF FRANCE IN THE 1400'S

XIII, he exemplified the Bench's proud tradition of courageous independence.[22a]   This record is symbolized in this Hall by the statue of the heroic Malesherbes, the Erskine of France, who dared to act as counsel for Louis XVI before the Revolutionary Convention, and himself met his royal client's fate at the guillotine two years later. Here, too, has been placed the inspiring monument to the Paris lawyers who gave their lives for their country in the World War.   And it was an impressive consummation of these traditions when in July, 1924, for the first time in history, the President of the American Bar Association

XV. 22—THE SALLE DES PAS PERDUS, IN PARIS
This is its popular name, "Hall of Wasted Time"

[*1005*]

XV. 23—The American Bar Association at the Palace of Justice, 1924

[1006]

and the President of the Paris Bar Association met and fraternized in the name of our common profession.[23] Yet the popular epithet for this Hall is a cynical reflection on that same profession; for it signifies that going to law is in popular esteem merely time and money wasted for the client.

7. Meanwhile, by the third century after Irnerius, Italy's star of leadership in Roman law was waning. During the 1200's, 1300's, and 1400's, the thousands of foreign students had gone back North and West carrying the new advanced ideas of Roman Law. Italian doctors of law were invited abroad. Faculties of law sprang up in Spain, France, Germany, and the Netherlands.

Even as far north as England, indeed, some of the Bologna jurists had early wandered, bringing the new science. Doctor Vacarius, of Bologna, about A. D. 1150, the very next generation after Irnerius, came to England and taught law, probably at Oxford. The chronicler says that students both rich and poor flocked to hear him teach the Roman laws; and because the poor students could not buy parchment copies of Justinian's Code and Digest, he made a summary for them, containing all that a student would need to know,—*if* he knew it perfectly; and this was called a Summary of Law for Poor Students. Another chronicler tells us that English University students at this

[*1007*]

period had abandoned philosophy for the study of Roman law. The Bologna jurists' books also were widely circulated in England. Many famous passages of Justinian's Digest, quoted literally in Azzo's book, we find again, word for word, in Bracton's treatise; for we know that our English judge and first great author, Henry Bracton, about A. D. 1250, copiously used a Summary of Roman Law, by Azzo of Bologna, in composing his treatise on the Laws of England. Azzo of Bologna was called in his day "master of the masters of law"; he was so authoritative that the popular phrase ran: "Chi non ha Azzo non va al palazzo", which may be translated: "Unless on Azzo you prepare, the jurist's robe you'll never wear".

But Roman law was still too exotic for regions like England and Germany, where sturdy Germanic legal ideas were yet solid and pure. And so it was natural that in South France the new Roman law first found most fertile soil for cultivation. In the 1500's the primacy in Roman legal scholarship passed to France; in the 1700's to Holland; in the 1800's to Germany;[24] for, as political, intellectual, and commercial influences pushed gradually west and north the centre of European forces, so also the primacy in Roman law studies gradually shifted, from century to century, through four countries.

[*1008*]

XV. 24—Map Showing the Shift of Primacy in Roman Law Studies

8.   In France, the great name was Cujas.[25]   Roman law had in France by the 1500's become the fashionable study for the nobility.   At some courses, four thousand hearers are said to have attended,—incredible as this may sound.   New and improved methods of research and exposition had been devised, and Cujas was their greatest exponent.   The old style of Bartolus was called "mos

[*1009*]

XV. 25—Cujas

[1010]

Italicus"; the new style was now known as "mos Gallicus". The English jurist Duck wrote, in A. D. 1650, "Roman legal science, if it should perish in every other country, could be entirely reconstructed from French learning only". The School at Bourges, where Cujas taught, was then termed "the great market-place of legal science in Europe". When professors in Germany cited Cujas, they lifted their hats at the mention of his name. At Bourges it was the custom of his admiring students to form a procession and escort him from his house to his lecture, and back again.

In the house of Cujas,[26] the traveler may still contemplate the habitat of this unique scholar. His peculiar custom was to leave his books all around him on the floor of his study, to lie on his stomach as he read them, and to drag his short stout body across the room from one pile of books to the other as he took his notes.

XV. 26—THE HOUSE OF CUJAS

XV. 27—THE SENATE HALL AT LEIDEN UNIVERSITY

9. By the 1700's the primacy had passed northwards to the Netherlands. Of the Senate Hall[27] at Leiden University the German historian Niebuhr has said, "No locality in Europe is so memorable in the history of science". Hugo Grotius was learned in Roman law, though he left his imperishable mark on international law; his work on the Law of War and Peace, appearing in 1627, was placed on the Index Expurgatorius by the Pope (though recently taken off), yet it became the Bible of

[*1012*]

XV. 28—Noodt, Professor at Leiden

lawyers. But in the Roman law field the Netherlands at this time, under the scholarship of men like Noodt,[28] devised new methods. The "methodus Noodti", oftener termed the "elegant method", now became more fashionable than the "mos Gallicus" of France.

The Dutch influence reconstructed Scottish law. Long before this period, Scottish law students had begun to flock to Leiden to study the Roman law; and it was the political feuds with the English, and the proximity of Leiden, which resulted in Scotland almost completely Romanizing its law under Dutch inspiration. A Scottish

XV. 29—Parliament Hall, Edinburgh

jurist, speaking of the end of the 1500's, recorded that "those who are in daily practice in the courts consume their days and nights in learning the civil law of the Romans, and give their whole labours to the practising of it, neglecting the laws of their fathers."[d] And the Hall of Justice,[29] in Edinburgh (known as Parliament Hall), is today the only one in Europe (except Paris) where the barristers still keep up the ancient custom of meeting the attorneys and clients in this great anteroom to the courts.

10. But by the 1800's the primacy in Roman law studies passed to Germany.

As early as A. D. 1500, indeed, the new Roman law science had made its way into the German faculties, and was knocking at the doors of the courts. Hundreds of law students had gone to the law schools of Italy and of France during the 1200's, 1300's, and 1400's; for example, a single noble family of Germany in the 1400's sent seven of its scions to Italy for a doctor's degree in law. These men, trained in the new legal science, came back and spread its gospels. They took service with princes, and gave clever advice in the political struggles. They founded law schools; the first German faculty of law was organized at Heidelberg in A. D. 1498, four centuries after Irnerius; and others followed shortly. Soon these doctors of law were made judges by the princes.[30] The German emperor encouraged their Roman law, because it was imperialistic; and in A. D. 1495 he established the Chamber of Justice of the Holy Roman Empire; one-half of its judges might be princes, but one-half must be doctors of the new Roman law.

These new doctors sneered at the crude rules of thumb of the old Schoeffen-Court of lay judges (*ante,* Chap. XII).

[*1015*]

XV. 30—GERMAN APPEAL COURT, A. D. 1500

They cited the Romanesque texts in their opinions and ignored the local customs. The old Schoeffen, indeed, what with the introduction of written pleadings and Latin opinions, could no longer well understand what the suit was about; for few of them could read and still fewer could write. In the rivalry which ensued there was much bitterness. But the learned doctors of law prevailed. A trained legal profession grew up. As a culmination, we find the German Faculties of Law given the status of "amici curiae", or judicial advisers in law cases, and their opinions obtained the force of law.

[*1016*]

XV. 31—Carpzov, Professor and Judge at Leipzig

An opinion of the great Carpzov[31] illustrates the way this influence helped to bring in Roman law. Carpzov was a professor in the Law Faculty of Leipzig, and also chief of the Court of Schoeffen or lay-judges, as well as a member of the Court of Appeals. (This extraordinary man, by the way, is said to have pronounced twenty thousand death sentences in his judicial career, or about twenty a week; but was withal a very pious Protestant, and had read through the entire Bible fifty-three times). His printed opinion, or consilium, on a given case is seen[32] to be composed in Latin, and sets forth the reasons according to Roman law, citing largely the Digest of Justinian; then at the end, in the right-hand column, is the entry: "Thus decided the Schoeffen of Leipsic in Jan. 1644"; the text of this Schoeffen's judgment, however, is in German. Yet the copious italics for Latin law-terms show that even the court-records were yielding to the new Roman technique.

German legal learning in Roman law culminated with Savigny and Windscheid and Von Ihering in the 1800's.[33] The development had been slow; for, naturally, the pure Germanic rules of the North were slower to yield to the new Roman influence than the institutions of Italy and south France and Spain, which were already half Roman

78   Decifionum Illuftrium Saxonicarum

17 propter ejus defenfionem, † ob quam multa admittuntur, quæ regulis juris alias contrariori videntur, Dan. Molier. *ad Conft. Elect. 23, num. 13. part. 4.* Hyppolit. de Marfil. *in l. 1. §. fi quis ultimon. 89. & feqq. ff. de quæft. de quo dixi in pract. criminal. part 3. quæft. 115. n. 74. & 75.*

18   (2.) † Admittitur quoque examen teftium ad perpetuam rei memoriam in criminalibus, quando judex per inquifitionem & ex officio procedit, *dict. cap. quoniam frequenter. §. funt & alii cafus. ubi Gloff. in verb. regulariter. verf. & in caufa inquifitionis & Hoftienfis, num. 3. extr. ut lite non contefata.* Farin. *dict. quæft. 76. n.116.*

Nempe quia tunc'teftes recipiuntur pro informatione judicis, quæ regulis juris non fubjicitur; Sed licet judici procedere, etiamfi nec de delicto nec de delinquente conftet, hunc in finem, ut cognofcatur, an crimen certa in provincia commiffum, & quisnam autor iftius fit, quo tutius poftea fpecialis inquifitio formari queat, Angel. Aretin. *de malefic. in verb. Hæc eft quædam inquiftio n. 3.* Marant. *in fpecul. tit. de inquifit. num. 30. & feqq.* Erneft. Cothmann. *vol. 3. Reffponf. 30. n. 153.* Bartol. *in l. congruit, num. 3. ff. de offic. præfid.* Conrad. Lancellot. *de inquifit. n. 5.*

venimus 13. ff. de aur. & argent. §. fi tamen alienam 26. Inft. de rer. divifion. Caftrenf. in l. fi ita ftipulatus §. C.. yfogonus verf. qued nota. ff. de verb. obligat. Sixtin. vol. 2. confil. Marpurg. 7. n. 59. † Aliter quoque fi diceremus, fraus legi adinventa effet, cum nemo non criminaliter agens, annectere poffet petitionem civilem, ad hoc, ut teftes ftatim examinari poffent; at fraudi non eft indulgendum, l. in fundo 38. ff. de rei vendicat, l. cum hi. §. §. fi. cum his 20. ff. de tranfact.

22

Ita † *Scabini Lipfienfes ad requifitionem Joh.* 23 *Erich Huyns zu Helmftadt, Menf. Jan. An. 1644. (Verba Sentent. Hat Titius in Vollmacht Seji, wider Cajum wegen prätendirter Untreu. fo er, als in Kauffmannfchafft ihme Bediener, erwiefen haben foll, civiliter geflaget, nachmahls aber etliche Additionales übergeben, und fein Petitum unter andern fo weit geändert, daß er Cajum nunmehro principaliter Actione criminali, auff die ordentliche in Rechten gegründete Stroffe des Diebftahls, nachmahls auch und incidenter reftitutionem rerum ereptarum wolle belanigt haben, uff weil der Zeugen etliche zur See reifende Leute, hat er inftändig angefuchet, diefelbe noch vor der Kreigs-Befeftigung, ad perpetuam rei memoriam abzuhören, Als nun Cajum folchem fuchen widerfprechen,*

XV. 32—An Opinion of Carpzov

The opinion is composed in Latin, but the judgment
("sententia") is formulated in German

---

or more. And so it was not until the 1800's that Germany's turn came to stand in the forefront of Romanesque law. Windscheid's Pandects became a reference-book throughout Europe; some of Von Ihering's books went into twenty German editions and into nearly every language of civilization; and Germany's authority in Roman law studies became world-wide.

[*1019*]

XV. 33—Windscheid and Von Ihering

11. *Nationalization*

11. But during most of these seven centuries from
A. D. 1100 to 1800 Romanesque law had passed through
only two of its four stages; the remaining stages may
be briefly outlined:

Dates	Processes	Agencies
A. D. 1100 1200	I. THE RESURRECTION of Justinian's lost Book-Law	The Jurists of the Universities
1300 1400 1500 1600	II. THE ADAPTATION of it to the new social conditions of Romano-Germanic peoples and THE ADOPTION of it as a Common Law of western Europe alongside a thousand local laws	The Jurists and The Practitioners
1700 1800	III. THE NATIONALIZATION of these into Romanesque National Codes	The Jurists and The Legislators
1900	IV. THE EXPANSION of Romanesque principles over the World in other national Codes	The Statesmen and The Jurists

The first stage had been the Resurrection of Justinian's law.

The second stage had been the Adaptation of it in
practice to the new social conditions, and the Adoption of

it as a general or common law. But this "common law", as it was called, was only secondary; in practice, there were still a thousand separate jurisdictions whose local law had the priority over this common law (*ante*, Chapter XII). Each of these local law-bodies was more or less Germanic; only the secondary common law for all was Roman. How little the law of those days could yet be deemed national may be inferred from the fact that neither in France nor in Germany was there a professorship of French or of German law until about A. D. 1700.

In the third period, then, it remained to merge these into a single nation-wide system for each country. This new system would be neither Germanic nor classic; it would be Romanesque, in the same way that a well-known type of architecture has been termed Romanesque. And, most of all, it would be a unified national system.

12. This great task of nationalizing the law was first achieved in France in the early 1800's, but only after three centuries of effort.

Charles Dumoulin,[34] a fiery patriotic lawyer of the 1500's, had already dreamed of a single code for France. This most famous lawyer of his day was an embodiment of self-esteem; at the caption of his opinions he wrote: "Ego a nemine doceri possum", "Nobody can teach Me the law". But Dumoulin was one of those characters of

CHARLES DUMOLIN.
Avocat au Parlement.
Né à Paris sur la fin de 1500 Mort en xbre 1566.

B. Pinx.   Ficquet Sculp.

XV. 34—Dumoulin
"Nobody can teach Me the law"

[1023]

indomitable honesty who have made the Bar an honorable profession. When a certain powerful count had asked him for an opinion, in a cause which Dumoulin deemed an unjust one, he refused it; the Count threw him into prison—and Dumoulin still refused the opinion.

Dumoulin's dream of a national code was premature. But in the next century, about A. D. 1665, a partial success was achieved by that great minister of Louis XIV, Jean Baptiste Colbert,[35] a man of Scotch ancestry. Louis XIV aspired to be known as the Justinian of France, and Colbert was his Tribonian. Colbert has been by some historians termed the greatest minister in the annals of mankind. Within twenty years he had unified, nationalized, and codified five great fields of law,—Civil Procedure, Criminal Procedure, Commercial Law, Maritime Law, and Colonial Law. But he never lived to complete his career with a Civil Code.

In the next century, the 1700's, however, this task was brought nearer by Robert Pothier.[36] Pothier was professor at Orleans, but also served for fifty years on the bench. During the last twelve years of his life this extraordinary man wrote a comprehensive series of twenty-six separate treatises, covering the whole civil law. Voltaire had said, in sarcasm, that the traveler in France changed his law as often as he changed horses. But Pothier

XV. 35—Colbert the Codifier

[1025]

XV. 36—POTHIER, JUDGE AND PROFESSOR

In twelve years he wrote twenty-six treatises, covering the whole
French civil law, and preparing the way for Napoleon's
nationalization of the law

demonstrated that the civil law of France could be stated in the form of a single harmonious nationalized system. It remained then only to bring about political unity and centralized legislation, and this law of France could be codified.

13.   This was the achievement of the Revolution. The jurist Cambacérès,[37] in 1796, afterwards Second Consul and Minister of Justice under Napoleon, was the prime mover, with a draft for a national code, at the very opening of the Revolution.[38]   But dissensions blocked his plan. It remained for Napoleon, the man of autocracy, to weld with his hammer the conflicting interests; and after four years of legislative labors, the Civil Code was achieved in 1804, and the others a few years later; there were five in all,—Civil, Criminal, Commercial, and Civil and Criminal Procedure.   The chief figures who stand out in this final stage were Portalis and Tronchet,[39]—one the philosophic jurist, the other the skilled practitioner.

The composition of these codes was the most rational and thorough proceeding of its kind in all history up to that time.   Justinian's undertaking had been in comparison a superficial and mechanical task.   This one was a model of representative political method.   The entire bench and bar of France took part; scores of professional meetings were held; hundreds of reports were filed; the

XV. 37—Cambacérès, Minister of Justice Under Napoleon

CORPS LEGISLATIF.

PROJET

DE

CODE CIVIL,

PRESENTE

AU CONSEIL DES CINQ-CENTS,

Au nom de la commission de la classification
des lois,

PAR CAMBACERES,

DÉPUTÉ PAR LE DEPARTEMENT DE L'HERAULT.

A PARIS,
DE L'IMPRIMERIE NATIONALE.

MESSIDOR, AN IV.

XV. 38—CAMBACÉRÈS' DRAFT OF A CIVIL CODE

[1029]

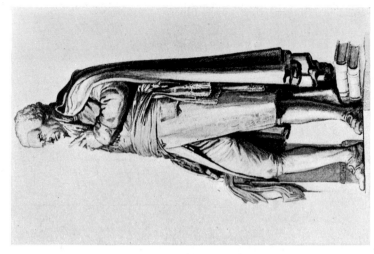

XV. 39—PORTALIS AND TRONCHET
Leaders in the composition of the French Civil Code

[1030]

XV. 40—Napoleon Receiving the Code

drafts were debated in successive stages in various legislative bodies. The printed proceedings on the codes fill
forty volumes.

Napoleon himself presided officially at many of the
debates, and his will shaped more or less of the code.[40]
In one case he directed the council to report out the draft
within fifteen days; but when it proved that the report of
the obstinate jurists went counter to his will, he ad-
journed the debates on that topic for three years, hoping,
though in vain, for a change of professional opinion. In
his later days, as a captive at St. Helena, he said: "My
glory is not to have won forty battles; for Waterloo's de-
feat will destroy the memory of as many victories. But
what nothing will destroy, what will live eternally, is my
Civil Code".

That code stands out as one of those few books which
have influenced the whole world.[41] The Code Napoleon
was soon translated into almost every language. It set
the fashion, and the other Romanesque countries of
Europe were ripe to follow. In all of them the task was
similar,—to extinguish the thousand local law-codes,
"fueros" in Spain, "statuta" in Italy, "keuren" in Netherlands, "stadtrechte" and "landrechte" in Germany and
Austria, "cantonrechte" in Switzerland; and to weld

CODE CIVIL

DES

FRANÇAIS.

ÉDITION ORIGINALE ET SEULE OFFICIELLE.

GRAND-JUGE ET MINISTRE DE LA JUSTICE

A PARIS,

DE L'IMPRIMERIE DE LA REPUBLIQUE.

An XII.—1804.

XV. 41—CODE NAPOLEON, FIRST EDITION

them with the Roman Common Law into a single Roman-esque system.

The first to complete the task was Austria in 1811; then followed Netherlands in 1838; Italy in 1865; Spain in 1888; Germany in 1896; and Switzerland in 1907.[42] Eight centuries had elapsed from the Resurrection of Roman law in the 1100's to the final Formulation of Romanesque law in the 1800's.

(IV) FOURTH PERIOD

14. But this was not the end of its destiny. Its fourth period was to arrive,—the period of expansion. This period of expansion was now to make it one of the modern world's three great systems.

The Islamic law had become a world-system through religious expansion; the original Roman law had spread by military conquest; the Anglican law by colonization. But the Romanesque system was not extended by conquest nor by religion nor by colonization. Two main influences shaped its destiny,—one scientific, the other political.

In the first place, every law-faculty in Continental Europe had for centuries been teaching Roman law as universal legal science. In the second place, the French Revolution had associated in men's minds national

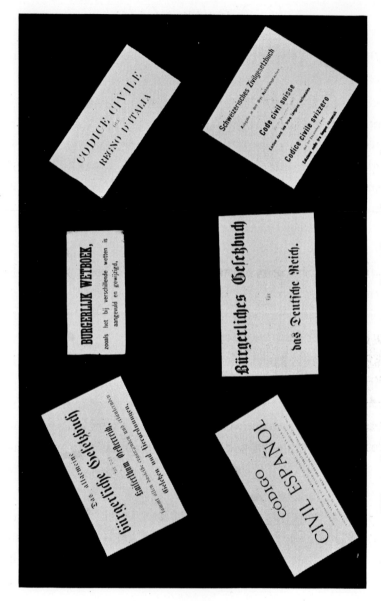

XV. 42—Codes of Austria, Netherlands, Italy, Spain, Germany, Switzerland

[*1034*]

codification with political reform. As a result of the former or scientific influence, the legal thought of all the remaining Continental countries was moulded more or less in Romanesque form;[43] in the case of Roumania, Hungary, Greece, Serbia, Bulgaria, this is notable; and even in the Germanic codes of Denmark, Norway, Sweden, and the Slavic code of Russia, modern Romanesque teaching is noticeable. As a result of the second or political influence, the new nations of Latin-America, on achieving independence in the early 1800's, proceeded to codify their national law; and as no Spanish code then existed, the Code Napoleon was naturally the chief model.[43] Scotland was already Romanesque; so, too, was Dutch South Africa, Quebec, and Louisiana; even Islamic Turkey and Egypt came to adopt in part the French legal scheme; and Japan in the 1900's used Romanesque models.

How marked is the community of legal ideas and phrases running through all these Romanesque codes may be seen by taking almost at random the parallel texts on some one subject: Art. 7 of the French Civil Code reads: "The exercise of civil rights is independent of citizenship, which is acquired and kept only as prescribed in the Constitution." Art. 6 of the Roumanian Civil Code reads: "The exercise of civil rights does not depend on

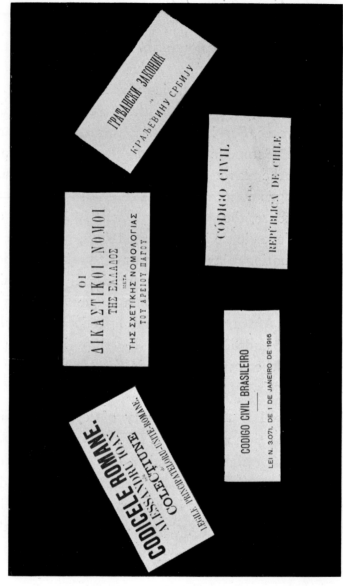

XV. 43—Codes of Roumania, Greece, Serbia, Brazil, Chile

citizenship, which can be acquired and kept only as prescribed in Art. 16 of this Code." And so on:

Parallel Texts from Civil Codes

France
Book I. Persons

Art. 7. "The exercise of civil rights is independent of citizenship, which is acquired and kept only as prescribed in the Constitution."
Art. 8. "Every Frenchman enjoys civil rights."

Roumania
Book I. Persons

Art. 6. "The exercise of civil rights does not depend on citizenship, which can be acquired and kept only as prescribed in Art. 16 of this Code."
Art. 7. "Every Roumanian enjoys civil rights."

Greece
Book I. Persons

Art. 9. "The enjoyment of civil rights is independent of citizenship, which is acquired and kept only according to the Constitution."
Art. 10. "Every Greek enjoys all civil rights."

Serbia
Preliminary

Art. 6. "Even an alien, dealing with Serbians or with other aliens in Serbia, may acquire rights under its laws."
Art. 5. "Every Serbian citizen, whether within or without Serbia, enjoys and is subject to Serbian law."

Chile
Book I. Persons

Art. 57. "The law recognizes no difference between the Chilean and the alien as to the acquisition and enjoyment of civil rights under this Code."

Brazil
Book I. Persons

Art. 3. "The law does not distinguish between citizens and aliens as to the acquisition and enjoyment of civil rights."
Art. 2. "Every man is capable of civil rights and obligations."

The most grandiose edifices of Justice in the modern world are monuments to that system,[44] which has transfused the pure Roman and Germanic systems into a new and composite one.[45] The elements supplied by the two

[*1037*]

x 5102   Bruxelles - Palais de Justice

XV. 44—PALACES OF JUSTICE AT ROME AND BRUSSELS

[*1038*]

XV. 45—PALACES OF JUSTICE AT BUENOS AIRES AND BUDAPEST

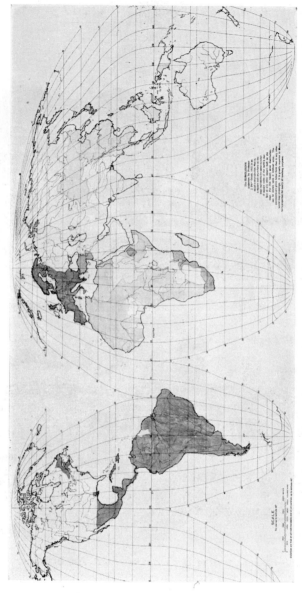

XV. 46—World-Map of the Romanesque System

The areas in light shading represent spheres of influence; those in darker shading represent a complete system of laws. The exact boundaries cannot be adequately shown on this map. The map in the Appendix attempts to show them more closely systems differ in ratio in different countries. Scholars agree, for example, that the French Civil Code, oddly enough, is more Germanic than it is Roman, while the German Civil Code is more Roman than Germanic. But both of these, and all of the others, may be termed Romanesque, in clear contrast to the other two modern world-systems, the Islamic and the Anglican.

The Romanesque system has belted the world from Quebec to Cairo, from Budapest to Buenos Aires.[46] Three hundred millions of people now live under it. Of the three world-systems of today, this one is the most extensive; it governs almost one-sixth of the world's inhabitants.

Sources

Sources of Illustrations

1. *Bologna.* From a photograph by *Pini*, Bologna.
2. *The Feudal Fighting-Towers of Medieval Pavia.* From a photograph by *Bruni-Marelli*, Pavia, of an old engraving.
3. *Irnerius.* From a photograph, made for the author in 1908, of the fresco by *Luigi Serra*, on the ceiling of the Town Hall in Bologna.
4. *Justinian's Digest.* From the photo-facsimile of the MS. in the Laurentian Library at Florence (cited *ante*, Chap. VII).
5. *Square of San Stefano.* From a photograph by *Pini*, Bologna.
6. *Law Lecturer and His Class.* From a photograph, by the *Emilia Co.*, Bologna, of the relief on the sarcophagus of Pietro Canonici, lecturer on Civil Law, in the Civic Museum at Bologna.
7. *Bologna Student Records (title-page).* From the reproduction of a record of A. D. 1502, in "Atlante paleografico artistico", plate CV, ed. *F. Carta* et al. (Torino, Bocca, 1899), in the Chicago Art Institute.
8. *Bologna Student Records (interior page).* From the reproduction in *E. E. James*, "Bologna, Its History, Antiquities, and Art", p. 176 (London, Frowde, 1909).
9. *Escutcheons of Nation-Captains.* From a photograph obtained at Padua.
10. *Tomb of a Jurist.* From a photograph, by *Pini*, Bologna, of the tomb of Rolandino dei Passagieri.
11. *Gloss on Justinian's Digest.* From p. 8 of a 1549 edition of the Digest, published by Hugo a Porta at Lyon.
12. *Justinian's Code.* From the title-page of the Koberger edition of 1488.
13. *Bartolus' Treatise on Alluvion.* From p. 144b of Bartolus' "Consilia", ed. 1552.
14. *Bartolus' Opinion on the Wine-Sale Statute.* From p. 200 of Bartolus' "Consilia", ed. 1552.
15. *Bartolus.* From an old engraving, anonymous.
16. *Palace of Justice at Ferrara.* From a photograph by *Lunghini & Bianchini*, Ferrara.
17. *Palace of Justice at Padua.* From a photograph by *Mattiozzi*, Padua.
18. *Palace of Justice at Rouen.* From photographs obtained in Rouen.
19. *Palace of Justice at Paris.* From a photograph in *H. Stein*, "Le Palais de Justice et la Sainte Chapelle", p. 137 (Paris, Longuet, 1912).

20. *Session of Supreme Court, Paris.* From a photograph made for the author by *Giraudon*, Paris, of the painting by *Pierre Dumesnil*, at Versailles.

21. *The Tribunal of the Terror.* From a drawing etched by *Duplessi-Bertaux*.

22. *Salle des Pas Perdus.* From an old engraving, anonymous.

22a. *A Chancellor of France.* From an old lithograph, anonymous.

23. *The American Bar Association in the Palais de Justice.* From a photograph furnished by *Wm. D. Guthrie*, Esq., of New York, spokesman of the delegation in 1924.

24. *Map Showing the Shift of Primacy.* Prepared by the author from J. Paul Goode's Homolosine Projection Map, 101 H. C.

25. *Cujas.* From an old engraving by *Ratmann*.

26. *House of Cujas.* From a photograph by *Laussedat*, Chateaudun.

27. *Senate Hall at Leiden University.* From a photograph furnished by Prof. C. Van Vollenhoven, of Leiden, 1924.

28. *Noodt.* From an old lithograph, anonymous.

29. *Parliament Hall, Edinburgh.* From a photograph, obtained in Edinburgh, of a drawing by an unidentified artist.

30. *German Appeal Court, A. D. 1500.* From an old woodcut reproduced in *Henne Am Rhyn*, "Deutsche Kulturgeschichte", vol. II, p. 56 (cited *ante*, Chap. XII).

31. *Carpzov.* From an old engraving, by *Dürr*, of the painting by *Steger*.

32. *Opinion of Carpzov.* From his "Opus Decisionum", p. 78, ed. 1729.

33. *Windscheid, Von Ihering.* From photographs obtained in Germany.

34. *Dumoulin.* From an old engraving, by *Ficquet*, found at Tours.

35. *Colbert.* From an old engraving by *Nanteuil*.

36. *Pothier.* From an old engraving of the painting by *LeNoir*.

37. *Cambacérès.* From a lithograph by *Delpech* of the painting by *Maurer*.

38. *Cambacérès' Draft.* From the title-page of "Projet de Code Civil", year IV.

39. *Portalis* and *Tronchet.* From engravings by *Mallin*, loaned by Mr. Edward Hertzberg, of Chicago.

40. *Napoleon Receiving the Code.* From an engraving, loaned by Mr. Hertzberg of Chicago, of the painting by *Philippoteaux*.

41. *Code Napoleon, First Edition.* From the title-page of the 1804 edition.

42, 43. *Codes of Austria, Roumania, etc.* From the title-pages of the books.

44, 45, 46. Palaces of Justice in
  Rome: from photographs by *Alinari*, Rome, taken for the author.
  Brussels: from a photograph by the *Photoglob Co.*, Zürich.
  Budapest: from a photograph by *Taussig*, Budapest.
  Buenos Aires: from a photograph furnished by the *Publisher's Photo Service*, New York.

47. *World-Map of the Romanesque System.* Prepared by the author, using J. Paul Goode's Homolosine Projection Map 101 H. C. (University of Chicago Press, 1923).

Sources of Documents Quoted in Text

a. Earliest Law Diploma. Translated from the text as given in *F. C. v. Savigny*, "Geschichte des römischen Rechts im Mittelalter", 2d ed., 1850, vol. I, Appendix.

b. Student Records at Padua. Translated from the reprint, ed. *Brugi*, of the Annals, covering A. D. 1555-1601, of the "Nazione Germanica dei Legisti nello Studio di Padova", in "Monumenta Storica", vol. XXI, 1st ser., "Documenta", vol. XV, p. 7 (Padua, Reale Deputazione Veneta di Storia Patria, 1912).

c. Wine-sale Opinion. See No. 14, *supra*.

d. Scottish students of Roman law. From Sir *John Skene*, as quoted in Holdsworth's "History of English law", vol. IV, 3d ed., p. 248.

General References

Continental Legal History Series (Boston, Little, Brown & Co.):

Vol. I: *Sundry Authors*, "A General Survey of Events, Sources, Persons, and Movements in Continental Legal History" (1912);

Vol. II, *Sundry Authors*, "Great Jurists of the World, from Papinian to von Ihering" (1914); chapters on Bartolus, Alciat, Cujas, Colbert, Pothier;

Vol. III: *J. Brissaud*, "History of French Private Law" (1912);

Vol. IV: *R. Huebner*, "History of Germanic Private Law" (1918);

Vol. XI: *Sundry Authors*, "Progress of Continental Law in the Nineteenth Century" (1918).

XV. Romanesque Legal System

Charles P. Sherman, "Roman Law in the Modern World" (Boston Book Co., 2 vols., 1917; this author's excessive claims for the wide influence of Roman and Romanesque law must be discounted).

Harold D. Hazeltine, "The Renaissance and the Laws of Europe" (Cambridge Legal Essays, 1926); "Roman and Canon Law in the Middle Ages" (Cambridge Medieval History, 1926, vol. V., chap. XXI).

Wm. S. Holdsworth, "History of English Law", 3d ed., vol. II, book III, chap. I, and vol. IV, book IV, chap. I (Boston, Little, Brown & Co., 1923).

Sir F. Pollock and *Frederic W. Maitland*, "History of English Law before the Time of Edward I", vol. I, chapters IV, V, VI (Boston, Little, Brown & Co., 1895).

Hastings Rashdall, "History of the Universities of Europe", vol. I (Clarendon Press, 1895).

Sir *Paul Vinogradoff*, "Roman Law in Medieval Europe" (London, 1909).

M. Fournier, "Histoire de la science du droit en France", vol. III, "Les universités" (Paris, 1892).

F. de Zulueta, ed. "The Liber Pauperum of Vacarius" (Selden Society, vol. XLIII, 1927).

Hugh H. L. Bellot, "Early Law Schools in London" (Law Mag. & Rev., 5th ser., 1911, vol. XXXVI, p. 257).

Chas. H. Haskins, "The Renaissance of the Twelfth Century," chapter on "The Revival of Jurisprudence" (Harvard University Press, 1927).

Lord *James Bryce*, "Studies in History and Jurisprudence" (Oxford and New York, 1901), Essay II on "The Extension of Roman and English Law throughout the World", reprinted in Vol. I of "Select Essays in Anglo-American Legal History" (Boston, 1907).

THE
ANGLICAN
LEGAL SYSTEM

XVI

The Anglican Legal System

(I) Building a Common Law

1. Diverse racial and feudal elements.

2. Unification—Insular location—William I, Henry II, Edward I.

3. Instinct for law and order—Bracton—Guilds of lawyers—Inns of Court—Yearbooks.

(II) Rejecting the Romanesque Law

4. Legal patriotism — Littleton, Fortescue, Coke.

5. A strong legal profession—Inns of Court.

(III) Cosmopolitanization and Expansion

6. Crudity of the 1400's.

7. Science and learning of the 1600's—Coke, Bacon, Selden.

8. Commercial and colonial expansion — Mansfield, Blackstone.

9. Anglican law belting the globe—The American Bar Association in London, 1924—Role of a professional class in maintaining a legal system.

XVI
The Anglican Legal System

O picture the history of the Anglican legal system is not within the present plan. But after what has been described of the other systems, something may be added to outline the answers to some natural questions.

Those questions are three: (I) Since England was settled by Germanic tribes, can Anglican law be deemed worthy of ranking as an independent system, not merely a branch of Germanic law? And (II) Why did not the resurrection of Justinian's law texts in the 1100's-1400's transform local law into Romanesque law, as it did in the rest of western Europe? And (III) How did English law come to be Anglican law, i. e. a world-system?

One may at least call to mind here the places, the men, and the documents that illustrate the answers to these three questions. And the story may be divided into three periods, corresponding to the three questions. The first period, A. D. 1100-1400, is the period of building a new common law of England. The second period, A. D. 1400-1600, is the period of rejecting the Romanesque law. And the third period, A. D. 1700-1900, is the period of becoming a world-system.

XVI. *Anglican Legal System*

CHART OF PERIODS: ANGLICAN LEGAL SYSTEM

Date	Phases	Events
1100	I. Period of	William I—Edward I
1200	BUILDING A COMMON	Bracton—Inns of Court
1300	LAW	Year-Books
1400	II. Period of	Fortescue—Coke—
1500	REJECTING THE	Inns of Court
1600	ROMANESQUE LAW	
1700	III. Period of	Coke—Bacon—Selden—
1800	COSMOPOLITANIZATION	Colonial Expansion—
1900	AND EXPANSION	Mansfield—Blackstone

(I) FIRST PERIOD

One could hardly have predicted that this island, successively overrun by Kelts, Romans, Danes, Saxons, and half-Romanized Northmen, was ever to have an indigenous unified territorial law of its own shaping. But several powerful circumstances, in the haphazard of history, coincided to produce that result very early.

1. In the first place, it was an island, and therefore isolated, and thus its peoples and customs tended to unity.

2. In the next place, its first Norman overlord, William I,[1] was a man who, in the multifold chances of the variation of species, happened to possess the compelling trait of political mastery and system. At the very outset, William conceived of his island as a strong centralized

[*1054*]

XVI. 1—William I

[1055]

XVI. 2—Domesday Book Chest

feudalism, not the usual feeble decentralized one. Domesday Book and Westminster Hall are the typical monuments of this idea.

Domesday Book (one may still see the chest in which it long reposed)[2] was his great measure for this centralization; it is called by Maitland "the most magnificent of William's feats". There is nothing like it in Continental Europe. It surveyed and listed, in A. D. 1085, all of William's new island possessions, for the purpose of taxation; and the theory back of it was that every acre of land was held, immediately or mediately, of him, the one central overlord.[3]

William, in the next two centuries, had two forceful successors like himself, Henry II and Edward I. These leaders, by their legislation, put an end in England to that kaleidoscopic conglomeration of petty separate baronial jurisdictions of law and custom which (as we

[1056]

XVI. 3—A Page from Domesday Book
The entry in the lower right-hand corner records lands in Herefordshire held by Turstin Fitz Rolf, who thus became lord of Wigmore Castle (still standing, in ruins). This Turstin carried the banner of William at the battle of Hastings

[*1057*]

have already seen, in Chap. XII) prevailed on the Continent for six whole centuries later. No common law could have grown up in England under such conditions. These men and their advisers put England six centuries ahead of the Continent by centralizing justice and nationalizing it.

The second typical monument of that centralization was Westminster Hall. Built originally in A. D. 1199 by William Rufus as a banquet hall, and occupied as a central court of justice after A. D. 1300, it is the oldest and the second largest court-house ever built in Europe,—two hundred and ninety feet long, seventy feet wide, and ninety feet high; and for six centuries it served as the chief palace of justice for England. During those ages it has witnessed the trial of an English King for his life;[4] of Wallace, the Scots hero; of Warren Hastings, an imperial governor;[5] and numerous other momentous dramas in the annals of English justice.

3. But a third great circumstance that made an English common law possible was again one of those chances in the variation of species that give variety to evolution; for Rollo's particular tribe of Norsemen that had settled in France and then came over to England must have possessed as a tribe in a marked degree the trait of law and order,—that rare trait which distinguished

XVI. 4—TRIAL OF KING CHARLES I IN WESTMINSTER HALL

[1059]

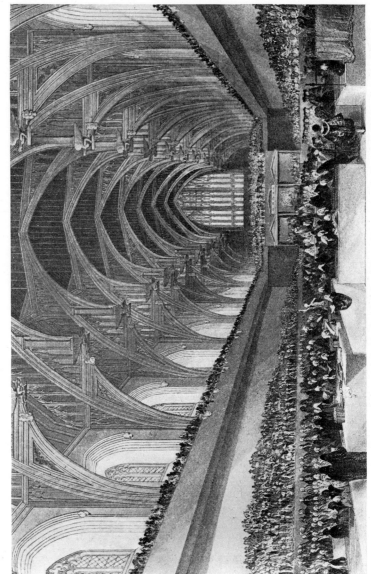

XVI. 5—Trial of Warren Hastings in Westminster Hall

[*1060*]

3. Norman Legalistic Instinct

Romulus' tribe in early Italy and Mohammed's tribe in Arabia, and by which those peoples stood out in history ever after. The Normans in England seemed to take naturally to law in all its phases, both legislative and justiciary. A foreign traveler in England, as early as the 1100's, records with surprise that "England was wholly given over to the study of law". At the time of the Conquest, almost every monastery possessed its legal adviser. The commissioners sent by William to supervise the administration of justice in the counties numbered "men learned in the Saxon laws." Crowds of civilians and canonists swarmed across the Channel for the express purpose of practising and teaching law. Archbishop Lanfranc, from the Abbey of Bec in Normandy, and William's great political adviser, had been in his youth a brilliant jurist at Pavia in Italy;[6] and his pupil and successor, Theobald,

XVI. 6—ARCHBISHOP LANFRANC
He was the chief legal adviser of William I

[1061]

when elected archbishop of Canterbury, attached to his household many young men who eagerly occupied themselves with legal studies; Peter of Blois, his secretary, has left a description:ª

"In the house of my master, the Archbishop of Canterbury, there are a set of very learned men expert in the rules of justice as well as other parts of prudence and knowledge. It is their constant custom after prayers, and before they dine, to exercise themselves in reading, in disputations, and in the discussion of legal causes. To us all the knotty questions of the kingdom are referred; which being brought forth into the auditory, where all the company assembles, everyone according to his rank whets his understanding to speak well, without wrangling or obloquy, and with all the acuteness and subtlety that is in him declares what he thinks the most prudent and sound advice. And, if it pleases God to reveal the best opinion to the lowest among us, the whole assembly agrees to it without envy or distraction."

About A. D. 1144 Theobald sent for Vacarius, the celebrated civilian of Mantua, who became the Archbishop's advocate, and no doubt lectured on law to the archbishop's young men. Many other monks devoted themselves, not only to Civil Law, but to the Common Law, both in court and in the schools outside as well as within the walls of the monasteries. It even became a popular saying that "nullus clericus sine causidicus."

One of the earliest products of this prolific interest in law was Bracton's great book, in the 1200's, "De Legibus Angliae."⁷ Bracton, a judge of long experience, wrote a

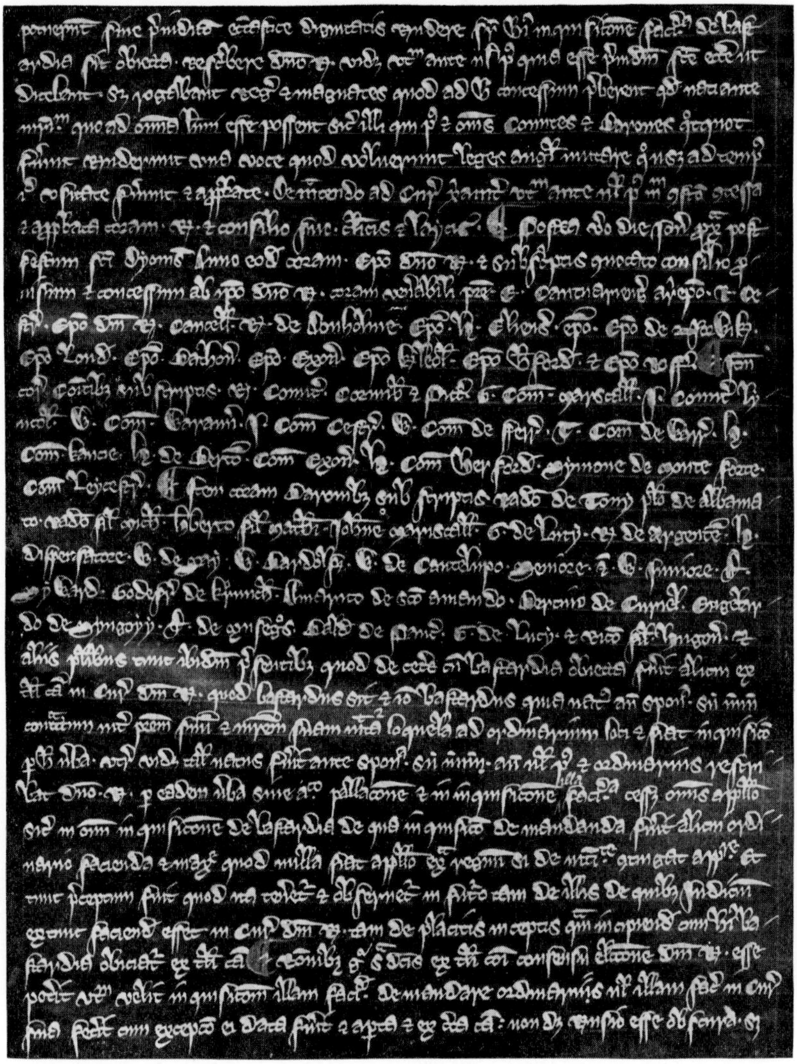

XVI. 7—A PAGE FROM BRACTON'S DE LEGIBUS

book which had wide vogue, and made it possible for the royal judges to unify the customary law of England. Bracton read and used Justinian's law-books, which had just been resurrected in Italy a century before. But he composed most of his text from his observations of cases decided in court. So his book represented in substance a native English, not a Romanesque, practice of law.

But what made such a practice possible? A profession of law, already developing in the Inns of Court. These Inns had begun early in the 1300's; they were the guilds of lawyers that grew up around the courts at London. Only four now survive,—Lincoln's Inn, Gray's Inn, Inner Temple, and Middle Temple;[8] the last two were so called from occupying the old quarters of the Knights Templars. But there were fourteen or more in all, at the height of their activity, and there were probably some two thousand members in all, each year.

The most distinctive result, then, of this Norman zest for law was that a legal profession arose at least two whole centuries before it did in Germany, Netherlands, and Scandinavia, the other pure Germanic countries.

The Inns of Court were guilds of lawyers with their apprentices, because every occupation was in those days organized in a guild.[9] The apprentices of law lodged and ate and studied together in these Inns.[10] They were like

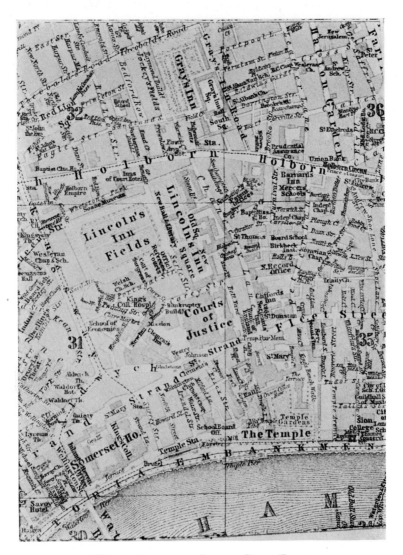

XVI. 8—MAP OF THE INNS OF COURT TODAY

XVI. 9—Lincoln's Inn: A Bird's-Eye View

the colleges at Oxford and Cambridge and the dormitories and fraternity houses in a modern American university. The incipient study of English law at Oxford and at Cambridge Universities was virtually abandoned. The Inns of Court became universities of law, and they were indeed so called by Chief Justice Fortescue, in the late 1400's, and by Chief Justice Coke in the 1600's. One of the courts—the Chancellor's Court—was for a time held in the very hall of one of the Inns, Lincoln's Inn.[11] Lectures were given and moot cases argued for the apprentices by lawyers of experience; and that experience was founded on practice in the courts.

XVI. 10—The Library, Inner Temple

[*1067*]

XVI. *Anglican Legal System*

XVI. 11—The Chancellor's Court, Held in Lincoln's Inn

For seven years, usually, this education must continue. A contemporary description of the educational program of the early 1600's exhibits the strong fraternal and professional bond that united apprentices and seniors in a common routine of almost monastic daily intercourse:[b]

[*Education at the Inns of Court.*] "Utter Barristers are such as from their learning and standing are called by the Benchers to plead and argue in the Society doubtful cases and questions, which are called Moots, and whilst they argue the said cases, they sit uttermost on the Forms of the Benches which they call the Bar. All the rest of the Society are accounted Inner Barristers, who for want of learning or time are not to argue in these Moots. Yet in a Moot before the Benchers, two of these, sitting upon the same Form with the Utter Barristers, do for their Exercises recite by heart the Pleading of the same Moot Case in Law French; which Pleading is the Declaration of the said Moot Case at large; the one taking the part of the Plaintiff, and the other of the Defendant. For the times of these Mootings, they divide the Year into three parts, viz. (1) The Learning Vacation, (2) the Term Times, and (3) the Dead or Mean Vacation. They have two learning Vacations, namely, Lent, which began the 1st Monday in Lent and continued 3 weeks and 3 days, and Summer Vacation, which began the Monday after Lammas Day and continued also 3 weeks and 3 days. And in these Vacations are the greatest conferences and Exercises of Study. In the Term Time the only Exercises of Learning are arguing and debating cases after dinner and Mooting after supper in the same manner as in the Vacations. The time between the Learning Vacations and Terms is called the Mean Vacation, during which time every day after dinner cases are argued as at other times, and after supper Moots are brought in and pleaded by the Inner Barristers, in the presence of the Utter Barristers which sit there in the room of the Benchers."

And these daily mootings—a rigorous form of educational method, which by the genius of a modern American, Langdell, has been restored into universal practice in law schools—occupied a formal and impressive status in the life of the Inns. Here is a chronicle of their procedure:[c]

[*A Mooting at the Inns of Court.*] "Immediately after Supper the Benchers assemble themselves in the Bay-window, at the upper end of the Hall; where, standing in order, according to their antiquity, there repairs unto them two Gentlemen under the Bar, whose turn it is to recite the Pleadings. Who, after a low obeysance, demand whether it be their pleasure to hear a Moot; and depart

[*1069*]

with an affirmative answer. Then the Benchers appoint two amongst themselves, to argue the Case, besides one of the Readers elect, who stands not in their assembly, and is to be allways one (as hath been said). Wherein note, that every man is appointed according to his turn as thus; The Benchers of this Society are divided into two several ranks or Classes; viz. the upper Classes, consisting of the Auncienty, and the lower of the Puisnes. Now at the first Moot of every tourn, the Puisne of the lower rank, and the puisne of the upper rank, are first to argue, and so afterwards of the rest in their turns. Which Order was (as it seems) devised, to the end every Bencher might once in a Term argue at one of those Mootes. When it is agreed on who are to argue, all the Benchers depart out of the Hall, leaving the rest of the Company there. The two Arguers walk a turn in the Court or Garden, untill the Hall be

prepared and made ready for them;[12] which being done, they return into the Hall, and stay at the Cup-board, demanding if the Moot-men be ready . . . . All parties being ready, the two Benchers appointed to argue, together with the Reader elect, take their places at the Bench Table, the auncient Bencher sitting in the midst, the second on his right hand, and the Reader elect on his left. Then the Moot-men also take their place, sitting on a Form, close to the Cup-board, and opposite to the Benchers. On the one side of them sits one of the Students, that recites the Pleading; and the other on the other side. The Pleadings are first recited by the Students;

XVI. 12—King's Bench Walk

XVI. 13—THE COURT OF COMMON PLEAS

The white caps, or coifs, seen on the heads of the judges and
some of the lawyers, are the insignia of the serjeants-at-law

then the Case put, and argued by the Barristers, and lastly by the Reader elect and Benchers, in manner aforesaid; who all three argue in English: but the Pleadings are recited, and the Case argued by the Utter-Barristers, in Law French. The Moot being ended, all parties return to the Cup-board; where the Moot-men present the Benchers with a Cup of Beer, and a slice of Bread; and so the Exercise for that night is ended. So that no man, though of never so great antiquity in the House, is privileged from keeping the Exercises of the House; those only excepted, which are past their Reading, and have never Read.''

In a view of the Court of Common Pleas (which Coke called the "lock and key of the law"), at the end of the 1400's, the white caps or coifs, seen on the judges and some of the lawyers, are the insignia of the serjeants-at-law, or senior leaders of the bar.[13] Now no one could be appointed a judge unless he was already a serjeant-at-law; and every serjeant-at-law, on first being made serjeant, must give a course of lectures on the law to the apprentices. And so we see the study and teaching and practice and judging of the law systematically organized in a hierarchy of the profession.

And the materials for knowing this practice were already copiously recorded in manuscript reports of cases decided by the courts—the Year-Books.[14] These were printed as soon as printing came into vogue, at the end of the 1400's; but they had long circulated in manuscript.[14a] These handbooks of the profession, by providing a com-

¶DE TERMINO HILLARIJ, ANNO   Fol. 2.
Regni Regis Edwardi tertij poſt conqueſtum primo.

E N vn briefe de Droit , la miſe de graund aſſiſe fuit ———
ioyn en tēps le autē Roy,⅋ bēe ſue de faire vener iiii.chiua-
lers deſlier le graund aſſ⁊ et puis la parol fuit ſans tour
per demiſe le Roy: ⁊ reſom a iii.ſemaygnes ore: ⁊ Merſt
fuit attorney pur le demandāt, et fiſt demaūder le tenāt al
prim iour, pur ceo quil ne vient nient, il prѣia q̄ le default
fuit recorb, & ſic fuit: et puis le quart iour il prѣya ſeiſin, ⅋
il auoit le graund Cape. Et Herle luy dit , que ſil recouer per
la default, le iudgemēt ſerra attrenche, auѣy ſerra le nonſuit le dōant aprѣes la
miſe. Et auѣy dit fuit, q̄ a vn original p̄ le default le tenant aprѣes le miſe ioyn,
iſſera le petit Cape: ⁊ le default dun part ⁊ dauter eſt perillous ꝛc. vt ſupra ,cuius
contrarium vſitur, pur ceo q̄ per def. abs le miſe home acard ſeiſin de terre.

Briefe de
droit,

XVI. 14—A PASSAGE FROM A PRINTED YEAR-BOOK

mon and continuous record of the practice, made possible
the development of a genuinely English law. They cover
nearly three centuries, from about A. D. 1270 to 1530.
During this whole period we find nothing comparable to
them, in any other country north of Italy.

Two typical cases, short and simple, from their
earliest period, are worth comparing with the contemporary court records in the other Northern peoples,—
Germany, Bohemia, Poland (*ante*, Chaps. XI, XII):[d]

[*A Year-Book Case A. D. 1308.*] "Robert Dumfraville brought
his writ of debt against Richard of Lonstede and demanded a hundred marks, in which [the defendant] had bound himself in case
he should not deliver a certain writing to [the plaintiff] on a certain
day, on which day [default was made].

[*1072*]

"*Westcote* [for defendant]. To this writ he ought not to be answered, for we have often tendered you the writing, and do so still. See it here! And always we have been ready, etc. We demand judgment.

"*Passeley* [for plaintiff]. You did not tender it on the day named in the writing whence our action arises. Judgment, whether we ought not to be answered.

"*Herele* [for defendant]. We also pray judgment, for you cannot deny that we have tendered and still tender the writing, and are ready, etc.; and you cannot show that you were damaged for

XVI. 14*a*—A YEAR-BOOK
MANUSCRIPT

want of the writing: judgment. And on the day when we ought to have delivered it and for a quarter of a year afterwards we were in the East, and we left the writing at home with our wife for delivery to you.

"*Passeley* [for plaintiff]. If the writing were unconditional, your answer would serve for any free man; but the writing is conditional, and the condition gives us an action to demand this debt for an unfulfilled condition; and that it is unfulfilled [the defendant] cannot deny. We demand judgment as before.

"BEREFORD, J. You demand this debt because the writing was not delivered, and he says that before now he has tendered it, and that he was always ready, and that he tenders it now. Therefore it is well that you receive it. Moreover, this is not, properly speaking, a debt; it is a penalty; and with what equity (look you!) can you demand this penalty?

"*Passeley.* [The plaintiff] is here by attorney, and the attorney is here to receive the hundred marks.

"BEREFORD, J. [According to you then] you were appointed attorney to win only, and not to lose.   I do not believe that he who received you [as attorney] received you in that form.   Therefore accept the [tendered] writing.

"*Passeley.* I cannot do that unless under a judgment of the court. If the law will suffer it, we will do it gladly.

"BEREFORD, J. Were you to remain asking for our judgment, you would not come by your debt these seven years, for a judgment of the law is not to be given in that sort of way."

In this second case, two points of law are debated, and the judge's remark shows how the law was developing by precedents:

[*A Year-Book Case: Covenant of an Infant.*]   Year Book 12 Richard II (1388), No. 5, Eldrich v. Quylter: "A man brought a writ upon the statute of laborers against another in London, and made declaration by Huls how one B. was retained in his service at the feast of St. John the Baptist in the tenth year to serve him for two years, and the said B. was in his service until the feast of All Saints then next ensuing; that he departed out of his service, and the defendant detains him, etc.

"*Gascoigne,* for the defendant, demanded judgment of his declaration since he has not said that he requested him, so that he has not assigned any wrong in him, wherefore he demanded judgment, etc.

"*Huls.* And we demand judgment, and we pray our damages, for default of response.

"*Gascoigne.* He has assigned a tort, that he retains him, which tort it is necessary for him to pursue in his declaration and to allege that he requested him etc. so that if he had retained him *after* the request, then he did a tort, which he has not alleged in his declaration, wherefore judgment, etc.

"*Wadham* [on the same side]. Without a request it is not a tort, because this is the statute 'Licet saepius requisitus'.

"THIRNING, J. [to *Gascoigne*]. I marvel at you that you dwell so long upon such a novel matter, that never has been seen before this hour, because a thousand declarations of that kind have been made here and held good, wherefore you may take whatever response you choose, etc.

"Wherefore *Gascoigne.* Then we say that the defendant is resident in the vill etc. in the county of E., and we say that this same one who he supposes was retained with him was the son of the defendant and his heir apparent, and departed from him at which time he was only of the age of ten years, nor was he more than ten years old at the time he was retained and besides we say that when he departed from him he was only of the age of eleven years, nor is he more now, wherefore he departed and returned to his father, and we demand judgment since he is of such an age if you should have this action.

"*Huls.* We say that at the time that he made covenant with us to serve us he was twelve years old and more and 'potens in corpore', in which case he was of an age to make a covenant, wherefore since you have admitted the retainer, we demand judgment, and we pray our damages.

"*Gascoigne.* And we demand judgment, since you have admitted that he was only of the age of twelve years, and so of such age that he cannot legally make a covenant for the tenderness of his age, wherefore judgment if you can maintain an action against us.

"And so to judgment."

XVI. 15—Westminster Hall

[1076]

4. *Legal Patriotism*

And so, what with William and his successors, and Domesday Book, and Westminster Hall,[15] and Bracton, and the Inns of Court, and the Year-Books, the close of the 1400's finds England with a single unified common law of its own,—a distinctive one, not merely a branch of the crude Germanic system.

This marks a first period, answering our first question.

(II) Second Period

But now, passing to the second question, Why did not English law succumb to the great flood of Romanesque law which gradually overwhelmed Germanic law elsewhere in western Europe after A. D. 1200?

The answer to this is found mainly in two ideas,— national patriotism, and a strong legal profession practising a unified common law.

4. The first idea is typified in Fortescue[16] and Coke. These men patriotically championed the native legal system. The spread of the Romanesque law on the Continent in the 1400's- 1500's was associated with

XVI. 16—Chief Justice Fortescue

the imperial plans of Charles V and the Papacy's claims of universal jurisdiction; and so the same political patriotism which supported Henry VIII's break with the Papal system was matched by a legal patriotism which inspired a devotion to the English legal system.

Chief Justice Fortescue's book, De Laudibus Legum Angliae, written about A. D. 1463, a popular book for laymen, was composed in praise of the laws of England; it invoked juristic patriotism, and pointed out the defects of the rival system.

In the next century another chief justice, Sir Edward Coke,[17] equipped with prodigious learning, and blessed with aggressive energy, set himself to rout the invasion of Continental law-learning, which was then at its height in England. How real was this conflict of systems may be illustrated by a single incident,—an entertaining literary duel:

XVI. 17—Chief Justice Coke

Chief Justice Littleton's famous book on Tenures, published in A. D. 1481, was the first book on English law ever printed.[18]   It was rather crude, compared with the Romanesque law-books of the day. It began with the celebrated sentence, "Tenant in fee simple is he which hath lands or tenements to hold to him and to his heirs forever". (Littleton's Tenures was almost memorized by the lawyers for three centuries thereafter; and in the 1700's a metrical version of this first sentence ran thus:

Fee simple.

 Enant in fee simple is he which hath Lands or Tenements to hold to him and to his heires forever : and it is called in Lattine, Feodum simplex : for Feodum is called inheritance, and Simplex is as much to say as lawfull or pure, and so Feodum simplex, is as much to say, as lawfull or pure inheritance : for if a man will purchase Lands or Tenements in fee simple, it behoveth him to have these words in his purchase, To have and to hold unto him and to his heires : for these words (his heires) make the estate of inheritance Anno 10. Henrici 4. fol 38 for if any man purchase Land in these words: To have and

XVI. 18—LITTLETON'S TENURES, PAGE 1

"Tenant in fee simple is he,
   And needs neither to shake nor shiver
   Who has his lands free from demands
   To him and his heirs forever.")

Now Sir Edward Coke's first great book was a commentary upon Littleton's book; he called it "Part One of the Institutes";[19] and Coke in his Preface had said that this book of Littleton's was "the most perfect and absolute work that ever was written in any humane science"! But the great French Romanesque jurist, Hotman, who visited England and at Queen Elizabeth's invitation was offered a position at Oxford, had publicly sneered at this same book of Littleton's; *he* called it a "clumsy, disorderly, and senseless piece of jargon"! This was a Romanesque lawyer's opinion of English law. And to this sneer Coke replied in kind. So it is easy to imagine the fervor with which the battle of the systems continued.

5. But the battle was a losing one from the start, for the Romanesque system. Here again, the Inns of Court typify the reason.[20] In the other Germanic regions, on the Continent, there was, as yet, no legal profession, no

XVI. 19—COKE UPON LITTLETON, FIRST EDITION

XVI. 20—CHANCERY LANE: GATEWAY TO LINCOLN'S INN

law schools, and no unified common law (*ante*, Chap. XII). There was thus no power sufficient to resist the inroads of the new hordes of doctors of law from Italy and France, bringing a highly developed science of a new common law of Rome.   In England, on the other hand, this same period found English law already long unified, and technically studied and taught by a strong professional fraternity.   "Taught law is tough law", said the modern English historian Maitland; that is one of the greatest truths in the history of law.   The Inns of Court[21] were the fortress from which an army of professional devotees fought stubbornly in defence of English law.

XVI. 21—Middle Temple Library and Gardens

XVI. 22—MIDDLE TEMPLE HALL

Moreover, this army represented the ruling class, socially
and politically, and always had
done so, since Norman times.
"Only the sons of gentlemen",
said Fortescue in his book,
"do study the law in these
hostels; there is scarce an eminent lawyer who is not a gentleman by birth and fortune".
The great traditions of famous
names cluster about all these
Inns of Court.[22]   In the Hall
of the Middle Temple, Shake-

XVI. 23—MIDDLE TEMPLE LANE

speare's Twelfth Night received its first performance. In
the Middle Temple lodgings[23] lived Plowden, Coke, Eldon,
Campbell, Charles Russell, as well as Addison, Fielding,
DeQuincey, Sheridan, Sir Walter Raleigh, Tom Moore.
And in Brick Court lived Thackeray, Goldsmith, and
Blackstone himself.   The Temple also claimed an American colonist, Middleton of South Carolina, who was afterwards Chairman of the Committee of Five at Philadelphia
to draft the Constitution of the United States. With the
Inner Temple[24] are linked the names of Littleton, Ellen-
borough, Thurlow, Samuel Warren (author of "Ten Thou-

XVI. 24—INNER TEMPLE HALL

sand a Year") and William Murray Lord Mansfield. And in Mitre Court Charles Lamb once lived. Originally the lawyers received their clients in the Temple Church,[25] each lawyer standing at his special pillar, just as they used to in the Palais de Justice at Paris. Lincoln's Inn counts among its past members William Penn, Tennyson, Oliver Cromwell, Daniel O'Connell, Brougham, Erskine, Disraeli, and Gladstone,—a brilliant galaxy. Mr. Tulkinghorn's chambers, in "Bleak House", were in Lincoln's Inn. And in a quaint corner of Staple Inn[26] Dr. Johnson once lived; but that is no longer a lawyer's building.

[*1084*]

5. Inns of Court

XVI. 25—Temple Church   XVI. 26—Staple Inn

Thackeray's classical description of the Temple, when Arthur Pendennis, the embryo barrister, began his career there, a century ago, depicts for future generations the esoteric professionalism of life in the Inns of Court:[e]

"The Knights of the Temple. Colleges, schools, and Inns of Court still have some respect for antiquity, and maintain a great number of the customs and institutions of our ancestors, with which those persons who do not particularly regard their forefathers, or perhaps are not very well acquainted with them, have long since done away. A well-ordained workhouse or prison is much better provided with the appliances of health, comfort, and cleanliness, than a respectable Foundation School, a venerable College, or a

[1085]

learned Inn. In the latter place of residence men are contented to sleep in dingy closets, and to pay for the sitting-room and the cupboard (which is their dormitory), the price of a good villa and garden in the suburbs, or of a roomy house in the neglected squares of the town. The poorest mechanic in Spitalfields has a cistern and an unbounded supply of water at his command; but the gentlemen of the Inns of Court, and the gentlemen of the Universities, have their supply of this cosmetic fetched in jugs by laundresses and bedmakers, and live in abodes which were erected long before the custom of cleanliness and decency obtained among us . . . . . . There is Pump Court and Fountain Court, with their hydraulic apparatus; but one never heard of a bencher disporting in the fountain, and can't but think how many a counsel learned in the law of old days might have benefited by the pump.

"Nevertheless, those venerable Inns which have the Lamb and Flag and the Winged Horse for their ensigns have attractions for persons who inhabit them, and a share of rough comforts and freedom, which men always remember with pleasure. I don't know whether the student of law permits himself the refreshment of enthusiasm, or indulges in poetical reminiscences as he passes by historical chambers, and says, 'Yonder Eldon lived—upon this site Coke mused upon Lyttleton—here Chitty toiled—here Barnwell and Alderson joined in their famous labours—here Byles composed his great work upon bills, and Smith compiled his immortal leading cases—here Gustavus still toils, with Solomon to aid him.' But the man of letters can't but love the place which has been inhabited by so many of his brethren, or peopled by their creations, as real to us at this day as the authors whose children they were—and Sir Roger de Coverley walking in the Temple Garden, and discoursing with Mr. Spectator about the beauties in hoops and patches who are sauntering over the grass, is just as lively a figure to me as old Samuel Johnson rolling through the fog with the Scotch gentleman at his heels on their way to Dr. Goldsmith's chambers in Brick

Court; or Harry Fielding, with inked ruffles and a wet towel round his head, dashing off articles at midnight for the Convent Garden Journal, while the printer's boy is asleep in the passage. If we could but get the history of a single day as it passed in any one of those four-storied houses in the dingy court where our friends Pen and Warrington dwelt, some Temple Asmodeus might furnish us with a queer volume. . . . . .

"On the first-floor, perhaps, you will have a venerable man whose name is famous, who has lived for half a century in the Inn, whose brains are full of books, and whose shelves are stored with classical and legal lore. He has lived alone all these fifty years, alone and for himself, amassing learning and compiling a fortune. He comes home now at night alone from the club, where he has been dining freely, to the lonely chambers where he lives, a godless old recluse. When he dies, his Inn will erect a tablet to his honour, and his heirs burn a part of his library. Would you like to have such a prospect for your old age—to store up learning and money, and end so?

"But we must not linger too long by Mr. Doomsday's door. Worthy Mr. Grump lives over him, who is also an ancient inhabitant of the Inn, and who, when Doomsday comes home to read Catullus, is sitting down with three steady seniors of his standing to a steady rubber at whist, after a dinner at which they have consumed their three steady bottles of port. You may see the old boys asleep at the Temple Church of a Sunday. Attorneys seldom trouble them, and they have small fortunes of their own.

"On the other side of the third landing, where Pen and Warrington live, till long after midnight sits Mr. Paley, who took the highest honors, and who is a fellow of his College, who will sit and read and note cases until two o'clock in the morning; who will rise at seven, and be at the pleader's chambers as soon as they are open, where he will work until an hour before dinner-time; who will come home from Hall, and read and note cases again until dawn next day, when perhaps Mr. Arthur Pendennis and his friend Mr. Warrington are returning from some of their wild expeditions. How differently employed Mr. Paley has been! He has not been throwing himself away; he has only been bringing a great intellect laboriously down to the comprehension of a mean subject, and in his fierce grasp of that, resolutely excluding from his mind all higher thoughts, all better things, all the wisdom of philosophers and historians, all the thoughts of poets—all wit, fancy, reflection, art, love, truth altogether—so that he may master that enormous legend of the law, which he proposes to gain his livelihood by expounding. . . . . . .

"Pendennis enjoyed the Temple life with a great deal of relish . . . . A long morning's reading, a walk in the park, a pull on the river, a stretch up the hill to Hampstead, and a modest tavern dinner . . . . these were our young gentleman's pursuits; and it must be owned that his life was not unpleasant. In term-time, Mr. Pen showed a most praiseworthy regularity in performing one part of the law-student's course of duty, and eating his dinners in Hall. Indeed, that Hall of the Upper Temple is a sight not uninteresting, and (with the exception of some trifling improvements and anachronisms which have been introduced into the practice there), a man may sit down and fancy that he joins in a meal of the seventeenth century.[27] The bar have their messes, the students their tables apart; the benchers sit at the high table on the raised platform, surrounded by pictures of judges of the law and portraits of royal personages who have honoured its festivities with their presence and patronage.

"Pen looked about, on his first introduction, not a little amused with the scene which he witnessed. Among his comrades of the student class there were gentlemen of all ages, from sixty to seventeen: stout grey-headed attorneys, who were proceeding to take the superior dignity; dandies and men about town, who wished for some reason to be barristers of seven years' standing; swarthy, black-eyed natives of the Colonies, who came to be called here before they

XVI. 27—Dinner in the Temple

practised in their own islands; and many gentlemen of the Irish nation, who make a sojourn in Middle Temple Lane before they return to the green country of their birth. There were little squads of reading students, who talked law all dinner-time; there were rowing men, whose discourse was of sculling matches, the Red House, Vauxhall, and the Opera; there were others great in politics, and orators of the students' debating clubs: with all of which sets, except the first, whose talk was an almost unknown and a quite uninteresting language to him, Mr. Pen made a gradual acquaintance, and had many points of sympathy."

And so, returning to our theme, it is easy to understand that, though the Romanesque law was then scientifically superior to English law, the alien system had no real chance of victory against a native legal profession so strongly entrenched—and entrenchered!

Thus was English law predetermined to remain English and not become Romanesque; and our second question is answered. That question was: Why did not the resurrection of Justinian's law transform English law into Romanesque law, as it did the rest of Europe?

(III) THIRD PERIOD

But, thirdly and lastly, how did English law become a world-system?

6. Let us admit frankly that in Coke's day English law still retained much of the crudeness of Germanic law. Littleton's book, and the other English law-books of that day, could not be compared with the Romanesque ones on

the Continent. Let us recall, for example, that as late as A. D. 1571, when Coke was already at the bar, the English Court of Common Pleas actually allowed the title to a piece of land to be decided by the old trial by battle, with hired champions—"that monstrous birth of ferocity and superstition", as Hallam calls it; and the description of the scene, with the rules of procedure, in Dyer's Report,[28] reads very like that in the Mirror of Saxony, composed more than three centuries earlier (*ante*, Chap. XII). Such law could in that condition never become a world-law.

What made English law cosmopolitan?

7. Five names,—Coke, Bacon, and Selden, Mansfield and Blackstone—typify the new era ushered in by the 1600's. For it was indeed a new era. This period was, as Maitland calls it, "the heroic age of English legal scholarship"; and the first three above names illustrate it. The English legal profession, partly as a result of the competition with Romanesque law, now produced some scholars who in the early 1600's proceeded to put science and learning into English law.

Of Coke's work, something has been said. Bacon[29] applied to law the same powerful methods of science which he brought into other fields; and he was the first to discuss English law in universal terms. Selden[30] was, in John Milton's words, "the chief of the learned men re-

So the first verdict was affirmed, and the demandants barred in the attaint. And upon this the demandants brought a writ of right, and counted upon their own seisin in the time of the King and Queen, *P.* and *M.* &c. And *Paramour* chose the trial by battle, and his champion was one *George Thorne*; and the demandants *e contra*, and their champion was one *Henry Nailer*, a master of defence. And the Court awarded the battle; and the champions were by main-prise and sworn (*quære* the form of the oath) to perform the battle at *Tothill*, in *Westminster*, on the *Monday* next after the morrow of the *Trinity*, which was the first day after the *Utas* of the Term, and the same day given to the parties; at which day and place a list was made in an even and level piece of ground, set out square, *s.* sixty feet on each side due East, West, North, and South, and a place or seat for the Judges of the Bench was made with-out and above the lists, and covered with the furniture of the same Bench in *Westminster Hall*, and a bar made there for the Serjeants at law. And about the tenth hour of the same day, three Justices of the Bench, *s.* DYER, WESTON, and HARPER, WELSHE being absent on ac-count of sickness, repaired to the place in their robes of scarlet, with the appurtenances and coifs; and the Serjeants

XVI. 28—WAGER OF BATTLE, A. D. 1571

7. *Coke, Bacon, Selden*

XVI. 29—FRANCIS BACON,
BARON VERULAM

XVI. 30—SIR JOHN SELDEN

puted in this land"; another epithet for him was "the great dictator of learning to the English nation". His special field was the history of law, and his universal learning put him on an equal footing with the Continental jurists.

These English scholars did not borrow the Roman law wholesale, as the Americans have borrowed golf and its rules. Rather, they made over the English legal concepts so as to be cosmopolitan, much as Americans have used and adapted the classical European architectural forms in the skyscraping buildings invented by themselves. In the neat metaphor of Professor Holdsworth, the great English legal historian of today, the Roman law learning "was received in small homeopathic doses, at different periods, as and when required; it has acted as a tonic to our native legal system, and not as a drug or poison".

8. Meanwhile, by the 1700's, English traders and English colonies had begun to dot the world in both hemispheres. English commerce had become cosmopolitan. The conditions were ripe for expansion of the law. William Murray Lord Mansfield,[31] and a few other judges, now carried onto the bench the spirit of Bacon and Selden, and made English commercial law cosmopolitan.

And at this propitious moment, Mansfield's protégé, William Blackstone,[32] first a professor, then a judge, was inspired to expound in lectures this Anglican system. On June 23, 1753, appeared the epoch-making announcement of Dr. Blackstone's course of lectures on the Laws of England.[33]

This was the first time that lectures on the English common law had ever been delivered at an English university. The book that came out of these lectures,[34] in 1765-1769, was unmatched for lucidity of style, outside of France; and it soon went around the world, in the colonies. So great was the appreciation in the American colonies

XVI. 31—William Murray Lord Mansfield

XVI. 32—Sir William Blackstone

OXFORD, 23 June, 1753.

In *Michaelmas* Term next will begin

A

COURSE of LECTURES

ON THE

LAWS of ENGLAND.

By Dr. BLACKSTONE, of *All-Souls* College.

THIS Courfe is calculated not only for the Ufe of fuch Gentlemen of the Univerfity, as are more immediately defigned for the Profeffion of the Common Law; but of fuch others alfo, as are defirous to be in fome Degree acquainted with the Conftitution and Polity of their own Country.

To this End it is propofed to lay down a general and com-prehenfive Plan of the Laws of *England*; to deduce their Hiftory; to enforce and illuftrate their leading Rules and fun-damental Principles; and to compare them with the Laws of Nature and of other Nations; without entering into practical Niceties, or the minute Diftinctions of particular Cafes.

The Courfe will be completed in one Year; and, for grea-ter Convenience, will be divided into four Parts; of which the firft will begin to be read on *Tuefday* the 6th of *November*, and be continued three Times a Week throughout the Remainder of the Term: And the following Parts will be read in Order, one in each of the three fucceeding Terms.

Such Gentlemen as propofe to attend this Courfe (the Expence of which will be fix Guineas) are defired to give in their Names to the Reader fome Time in the Month of *October*.

XVI. 33—ANNOUNCEMENT OF BLACKSTONE'S FIRST LECTURES

[*1096*]

COMMENTARIES

ON THE

LAWS

OF

ENGLAND.

BOOK THE FIRST.

BY

WILLIAM BLACKSTONE, Esq.
VINERIAN PROFESSOR OF LAW,
AND
SOLICITOR GENERAL TO HER MAJESTY.

OXFORD,
PRINTED AT THE CLARENDON PRESS.
M. DCC. LXV.

XVI. 34—FIRST EDITION OF BLACKSTONE'S COMMENTARIES

that one thousand copies of the first edition were imported in the first two or three years; for the first American reprint, in 1771, fourteen hundred subscriptions were taken before the edition was printed; and some twenty-five hundred copies in all were sold in the American colonies alone before the Declaration of Independence. The colonies were ripe to receive it. There were no Inns of Court, no organized means of acquiring a mastery of the law; the great period of American law schools had not yet arrived; even the humble school at Litchfield was not opened till after the date of political independence, about 1782.[35] Over two hundred colonial lawyers had gone across the ocean to the Inns of Court for their education during the 1700's; in Pennsylvania alone, four of these men became Chief Justices of the State, after independence; and several of them sat in the Constitutional Convention.

9. Thus, as the colonies grew into commonwealths, the Anglican system, following them, expanded and was adopted and adapted to their needs.

The earliest forecast of this transplantation of law is seen in the plans for the very first colonial settlement—Virginia, in 1606; the King's Instructions to the Virginia Council tell them that "the disposing of all causes happening within the same" should be "done as near to the com-

9. Expansion

Buildings of The Litchfield Law School - 1784
(First in America), Litchfield, Conn.

XVI. 35—THE LITCHFIELD LAW SCHOOL, TODAY
But its restoration is in progress

mon laws of England and the equity thereof as may be."
Then, a century later, in 1720, when the colonies had
multiplied and were no longer an experiment, Mr. West,
attorney-general to the Board of Trade, formulates a
general principle, in a sonorous phrase of global augury:
"The common law of England is the common law of the
plantations . . . . . Let an Englishman go where he
will, he carries as much of law and liberty with him as the
nature of things will bear." Later, in 1763, when the
Canadian regions came under English domain, the royal

proclamation gives assurance that "all persons inhabiting in or resorting to our said Colonies may confide in our Royal protection for the enjoyment of the benefit of the laws of our realm of England." And on the very eve of the colonial revolution, in 1774, the Continental Congress, "asserting and vindicating their rights and liberties", deem it fitting to "declare that the respective colonies are entitled to the common law of England." Finally, in Australia, in 1828, the New South Wales Act (9 Geo. IV, c. 83) plants the principle in those far regions, by declaring that "all laws and statutes in force within the realm of England at the time of passing this Act . . . . shall be applied in the administration of justice . . . . . so far as the same can be applied within the said colonies." The broad identical result is summed up, in 1853, by Mr. Justice Story: "Our ancestors brought with them the general principles of the common law, and claimed it as their birthright; but they brought with them and adopted only that portion which was applicable to their condition."

And so, after three centuries of expansion, at Washington[36] a Supreme Court now typifies the legal thought of fifty federated Supreme Courts developing a United States Anglican law. At Ottawa,[37] a Canadian Anglican law is now interpreted by the Supreme Court of a dozen federated provinces. At Melbourne[38] an Australian

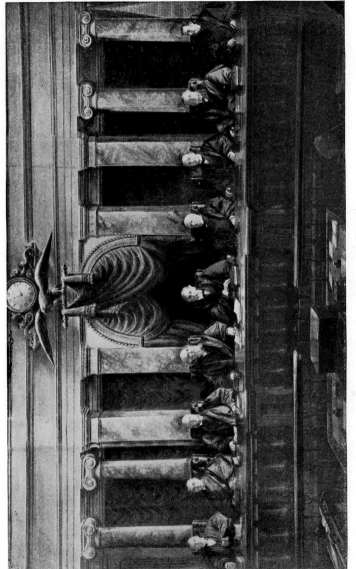

XVI. 36—Supreme Court at Washington

XVI. *Anglican Legal System*

XVI. 37—The Canadian Parliament Buildings

Anglican law is now expounded for a federated common-wealth. And in a modest building in Downing Street, London,[39] a cosmopolitan tribunal, known as the Judicial Committee of the Privy Council, is the arbiter for a hundred different legislative and judicial bodies of the Anglican system, in dominions, colonies, and dependencies located in the four corners of the earth.

The mere list of names of the more or less distinct entities that compose or affiliate with that Commonwealth exhibits the imposing variety of peoples who fall within the sphere of influence—either political, legislative, or judicial—of the British Anglican system:[f]

[*1102*]

XVI. 38—Supreme Court Building, Melbourne

XVI. 39—Privy Council Office, Downing Street

[*1103*]

XVI. *Anglican Legal System*

EUROPE

Scotland
Northern Ireland
Isle of Man
Channel Islands
  Jersey
  Alderney
  Guernsey
Irish Free State
Gibraltar
Malta

ASIA

Aden
Bahrein Islands
Borneo
  British North Borneo
  Brunei
  Sarawak
Ceylon
  Maldive Islands
Hongkong
India and Dependencies
  British Provinces
    Ajmer-Merwera
    Andaman and Nicobar
      Islands
    Assam
    Baluchistan
    Bengal Presidency
    Bihar and Orissa
    Bombay Presidency
    Burma

Central Provinces and
  Berar
Coorg
Delhi
Madras Presidency
Laccadive Islands
North-West Frontier
  Province
Punjab
United Provinces of Agra
  and Oudh
Indian States and Agencies
  Assam State
  Baluchistan States
  Baroda
  Bengal States
  Bihar and Orissa States
  Bombay States
  Burma States
  Centra' India Agency
  Central Provinces States
  Gwalior
  Hyderabad
  Kashmir and Jammu
  Madras States
  Mysore
  North-West Frontier
    Agencies
  Punjab States
  Rajputana
  Sikkim
  United Provinces States
The Straits Settlements
  Cocos or Keeling Islands

9. Expansion

Christmas Island
Labuan
Federated Malay States
Malay States not in the Federation
Weihaiwei
Mandated Territories
    Iraq (Mesopotamia)
    Palestine
    Trans-Jordan

AFRICA

British East Africa
    Kenya Colony and protectorate
    Uganda Protectorate
    Zanzibar
Mauritius
Nyasaland Protectorate
St. Helena
    Ascension Island
Tristan da Cunha
Seychelles
Somaliland Protectorate
South Africa
    Basutoland
    Bechuanaland Protectorate
    Southern Rhodesia
    Northern Rhodesia
Swaziland
Union of South Africa
    Cape of Good Hope
    Natal-Zululand
    The Transvaal
    Orange Free State

West Africa
    Nigeria
    Gambia
    Gold Coast
    Ashanti
    Northern Territories
    Sierra Leone
    The Protectorate
Anglo-Egyptian Sudan
Mandated Territories
    Tanganyika Territory
    South-West Africa
    Cameroons
    Togoland

AMERICA

Bermudas
Falkland Islands
Guiana, British
Honduras, British

Canada

Alberta
British Columbia
Manitoba
New Brunswick
Nova Scotia
Ontario
Prince Edward Islands
Quebec
Saskatchewan
Yukon
North-West Territories
Newfoundland and Labrador

West Indies
  Bahamas
  Barbados
  Jamaica
  Cayman Islands
  Turks and Caicos Islands
  Leeward Islands
  Trinidad
  Windward Islands
    Grenada
    St. Vincent
    The Grenadines
    St. Lucia

AUSTRALASIA AND OCEANIA
  Commonwealth of Australia
  New South Wales

Victoria
Queensland
South Australia
Western Australia
Tasmania
Northern Territory
Papua
New Zealand
Fiji

Pacific Islands

  Tonga
  Other Islands
Mandated Territories
  New Guinea
  Western Samoa
  Naru

Thus the Anglican system has belted the globe,[40] and has entitled itself to be classed as one of the three living world-systems,—that is, systems which have spread beyond the country and race of their origin. The other two are the Romanesque and the Mohammedan.

If we mark on the map with three colors the regions in which the respective systems not only hold exclusive sway but also have spheres of influence, leaving the white area to show the regions in which the native systems have not expanded, the result may be thus stated: The total population of the earth is some 1800 millions; the Anglican

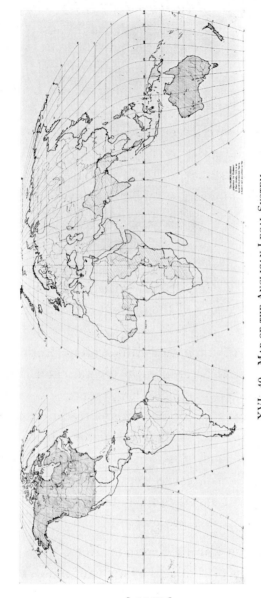

XVI. 40—MAP OF THE ANGLICAN LEGAL SYSTEM

The areas in light shading represent spheres of influence; those in darker shading a complete system of laws. In the Appendix Map (pp. 1144, 1145, 1146) the boundaries and degrees of influence are shown with more accuracy than is here possible.

[1107]

system now shapes the legal relations of some 300 millions of persons; the Romanesque, of some 300 millions; and the Mohammedan, of some 250 millions; or between the three, about one-half of the world's population in all.[41] All three systems have shown themselves strikingly adaptable, each in its own way, to its opportunities. Doubtless the most meritorious and adaptable will expand and survive the longest. And doubtless it depends largely on our profession to make our own system the most meritorious.

What the outcome of future centuries will be, none can attempt to predict. But, for the Anglican system, the most significant event of the present century was the visit of the American Bar Association to London in July, 1924, when lawyers of the Anglican system from the four corners of the earth assembled in Westminster Hall, in the oldest courtroom of Anglican law, where seven centuries bound them together in a common tradition and sentiment.[42] And, looking back on its history, it is possible to believe that the one most important thing that has enabled the Anglican legal system to survive and hold its own and expand has been its possession of a strong, fraternal, well-trained profession of the law.

And it seems fair to conclude, if we may generalize from this survey of the legal systems of many races, that

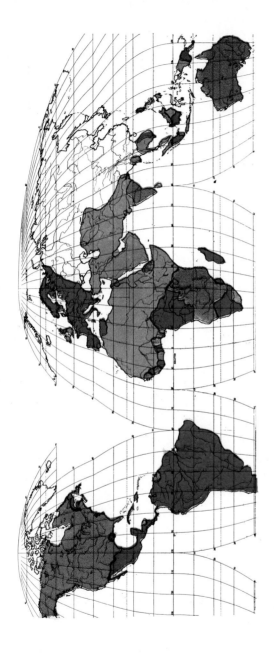

XVI. 41—Map of the Three World-Systems

In this map, as in those of Chaps. IX, XV, and No. 40 in XVI, the variant degrees of influence of the several systems cannot be accurately shown by single colors or shading. For a more particular discrimination of boundaries, see the Appendix Map

XVI. 42—The American Bar Association at Westminster Hall, 1924

the perpetuation of any legal system beyond the life of a particular political dynasty or of a particular race-stock can be guaranteed only by the development of a highly trained professional class.

But this thought leads to some other generalizations that concern the rise, progress, and disappearance of legal systems in general.

Sources of Illustrations

1. *William I.* From the illustration by *C. Laplante* in *F. P. G. Guizot*, "History of England", transl. Ripley, vol. I, p. 102 (Boston, Estes & Lauriat, 1876).

2. *Domesday Book Chest.* From a photograph by *Clark*, Chiswick.

3. *Domesday Book MS.* From a photograph made for the author in 1912 at H. M. Records Office, London. By an odd coincidence, the MS. book in its locked glass case happened in 1912 to lie open at the exact page containing the entry of the lands on which Wigmore Castle stood.

4. *Trial of Charles I.* From the illustration in *F. P. G. Guizot*, "History of England", vol. III, p. 108 (cited *supra*).

5. *Trial of Warren Hastings.* From an old engraving in the Elbert H. Gary Library of Law.

6. *Archbishop Lanfranc.* From a photograph, taken for the author, of the statue on the façade of Canterbury Cathedral.

7. *A Page from Bracton's DeLegibus.* From a photograph furnished by Prof. *G. E. Woodbine*, of Yale University, editor of the definitive text.

8. *Map of the Inns of Courts.* Prepared by the author from the plan in Karl Baedeker's "London" (1911).

9. *Lincoln's Inn.* From the illustration by *Home*, in *Headlam*, "Inns of Court" (cited *infra*).

10. *Inner Temple: The Library.* From the illustration by *Charles E. Flower*, published by *Raphael Tuck & Sons*, London.

11. *Chancellor's Court.* From an old lithograph by *Melville*, from a painting by *Shepherd*.

12. *King's Bench Walk.* See No. 10, above.

13. *Court of Common Pleas.* From an illustration reproducing an old MS., in Serjeant *Pulling*, "Order of the Coif", frontispiece (London, Clowes, 1884).

14. *Year-Book.* From an edition by Tottle.

14a. *Year-Book MS.* From the photograph in *Geo. F. Deiser*, ed. "Year Books of Richard II, 12 Richard II", p. 74 (Ames Foundation, Harvard University Press, 1914).

15. *Westminster Hall.* From an old engraving in the Elbert H. Gary Library of Law.

16. *Fortescue.* From the engraving in Blackstone's "Commentaries", 13th ed., vol. I, p. 251.

17. *Coke.* From an engraving by *Houbraken.*

18. *Littleton's Tenures.* From the edition of 1656.

19. *Coke Upon Littleton, First Edition.* From the edition of 1628.

20. *Chancery Lane: Gateway to Lincoln's Inn.* From an old lithograph, anonymous.

21. *Middle Temple Library and Gardens.* From a photograph by "A. R. W."

22. *Middle Temple Hall.* From a drawing by *Graham Clilverd* (1922), reproduced in the American Bar Association Journal, July, 1924.

23. *Middle Temple Lane.* See No. 12, above.

24. *Inner Temple Hall.* From a photograph by "A. R. W."

25. *Temple Church.* From a color-sketch by *Gordon Home*, in *Cecil Headlam*, "The Inns of Court" (London, Adam & Charles Black, 1909).

26. *Staple Inn.* From an old lithograph, anonymous.

27. *Dinner in the Temple.* From an old engraving.

28. *Wager of Battle.* From Dyer's Reports, p. 301b.

29. *Bacon.* From an engraving of the painting by *Van Somer.*

30. *Selden.* From an engraving by *Mytens* of the painting by *Chase.*

31. *Mansfield.* From the engraving by *Bartolozzi* of the painting by Sir *Joshua Reynolds.*

32. *Blackstone.* From a photograph, taken by Professor *W. S. Holdsworth* of Oxford, of the statue in All Souls College Library, Oxford.

33. *Blackstone's Announcement of Lectures.* From a photograph, taken by *Nelson Wettling*, Esq., of Chicago, of the original document in the Library of All Souls College.

34. *First Edition of the Commentaries.* From a photograph of the copy in the Elbert H. Gary Library of Law.

35. *Litchfield Law School.* From a photograph by *Karl Bros.*, Litchfield.

36. *United States Supreme Court.* From a lithograph published by the Boston Book Co. (1894), engraved by *J. Weston* from a photograph by *Notman*, Boston.

37. *Ottawa Parliament Buildings.* From a photograph in the *New York Times Magazine*, July 4, 1926.

Sources

38. *Melbourne Supreme Court Building.* From a photograph furnished by the *Chicago Transparency Co.*

39. *Privy Council Office.* From a photograph published in the *Green Bag* (Boston Book Co.), vol. VII, p. 65.

40, 41. *Maps of the World Systems.* Prepared by the author, using Goode's Homolosine Map No. 101 HC (University of Chicago Press, 1924).

42. *American Bar Association at Westminster Hall, 1924.* From the photograph published in the *American Bar Association Journal*, p. 572, August, 1924.

Sources of Documents Quoted in Text

a. Peter of Blois. As quoted by *Hugh H. L. Bellot*, in "Early Law Schools in London" (Law Magazine and Review, vol. XXXVI, p. 17, 5th ser., 1911).

b. Program of Education. From *Stow*, "Survey of London", 1598, as quoted by Ingpen, ed. of "Master Worsley's Book on . . . . the Middle Temple" p. 42 (London, 1910).

c. Mootings. From *Dugdale's* "Origines Juridiciales", as quoted in App. III to "Master Worsley's Book", p. 281 (cited *supra*).

d. Year Book Passages. From Y. B. 2 Edward II, A. D. 1308-9 (Selden Society Pub., vol. XIX, p. 58, 1904) and Y. B. 12 Rich. II, p. 108 (cited *supra*).

e. "Pendennis", chap. XXX.

f. List of territories in British Commonwealth. From the "Statesman's Year-Book", 1926.

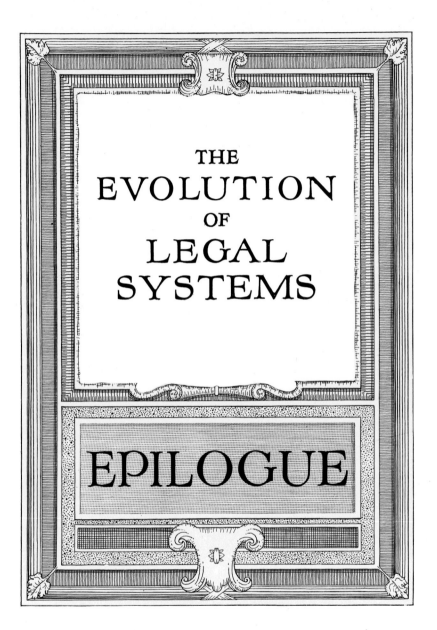

THE
EVOLUTION
OF
LEGAL
SYSTEMS

EPILOGUE

XVII.

The Evolution of Legal Systems

Legal systems as a whole, in contrast to
 specific legal ideas or institutions—General
 survey of the conception.

(*I*) *Comparative Law, in general*

(*II*) *Comparative Legal Institutions*

(*III*) *Comparative Legal Genealogy,*
 or Corporealogy

1. Corporeal method in comparative law.

2. Limited number of legal systems or bodies.

3. Problems peculiar to legal systems.

4. Causes of the creation, survival or disappearance of a legal system.

5. Existence of a trained professional class, as
 necessary to a legal system.

Epilogue:
The Evolution of Legal Systems

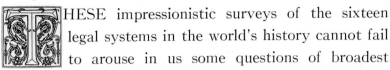HESE impressionistic surveys of the sixteen legal systems in the world's history cannot fail to arouse in us some questions of broadest scope. What gives rise to a legal system? What controls its destiny? What becomes of the specific institutions—property, contract, testament—within each system? Are all of them inherent in every legal system? Do they evolve at equal pace as a part of the system? Have the specific institutions common elements in all systems? Does the evolution of a single legal institution—e. g. mortgage—take place uniformly by itself for all systems, i. e. in cross-section, as it were, apart from the evolution of any given system as a whole?

To these and similar questions no answer will here be attempted. But heretofore, in studies of legal history and evolution, no emphasis has been given to the existence and growth of the world's systems as wholes —the subject of the foregoing surveys. And it is worth while to show here, in closing, the importance of this conception, as necessary before any final analysis of the evolution of specific legal ideas or institutions.

[*1119*]

And so (for those who care) the following broader survey of the whole field of the problem, in outline, is here offered.

(I) *Comparative Law, in General.* (1) The convenient but loose term "Comparative Law" has served to cover three fields scientifically distinct. When we lift our eyes beyond the sphere of the law that *is* (emphatically the only actual law for us, i. e. national law), and observe the systems of laws outside, present or past, we find three modes of activity for our thought of them.

First, we may seek to ascertain and *describe* the other systems, as facts. And, taking the term Nomology to signify the science of law in general, and Nomoscopy to signify the description of the facts of any system of law, let us call this branch Comparative Nomoscopy.

Secondly, we may seek to *analyze the policies* and relative *merits* of different legal institutions (e. g. the French and the English inheritance-rules, or the American and the English procedural rules) with a view to moulding legislation; let us call this branch Comparative Nomothetics; this is the main activity, e. g. of the Institute of Comparative Law at Lyon.

Thirdly, we may seek to trace the *evolution* of the various systems in their relation one to another in chronology and causes; let us call this branch Comparative Nomogenetics.

These three branches may use, to some extent, the same materials; and of course the first branch—Comparative Nomoscopy—is the one that furnishes most of the materials for all three. But the three represent different processes of thought, and are scientifically distinct.

The third branch, Comparative Nomogenetics—the evolution of the world's legal ideas and systems—is the one here concerned.

(II) *Comparative Legal Institutions.* Sir Henry Maine was virtually the first modern scholar to undertake to cultivate Comparative Law in general. Post, coming a little later, also advanced it, in other parts of the field. In the next generation, Dareste, Revillout, Kohler, and others, copiously enriched it. But these, and indeed most of the modern workers, have kept chiefly in the field of what is called above Nomoscopy; i. e. they have *described* other systems or institutions, but have not undertaken to trace their evolution, or *genetics*, comparatively. Sir Henry Maine's works, however, were almost all genuinely nomogenetic, though in the limited scope of four or five systems (Hindu, Greek, Roman, Keltic). As an example of an attempt to treat a single institution on a broader scope of evolutionary comparison (ten systems) may be cited the present writer's essay on "The Pledge-Idea; a Study in Comparative Legal Ideas".[1] And the necessary conditions (never yet fulfilled by any scholar) on which complete studies must be based have been suggested by the present writer in his essay on "Problems of the Law's Evolution."[2]

Naturally, in Sir Henry Maine's day, the extant materials for study of other systems were limited. But within the last generation the realms of archaeology, epigraphy, papyrology, philology, "et id omne genus", have vastly enlarged; so that today there remain virtually no civilizations unrevealed in available materials for study. Nor is it likely (except for the Hittite and possibly the early American peoples) that any more legal systems will be brought to light.

(III) *Comparative Legal Genealogy, or Corporealogy.* And this brings us to the next point; which is that hitherto there has been little or no consideration given to all these systems as *whole systems*, from the comparative point of view. Virtually all of the students (of course, Mazzarella, and one or two others, are exceptions) of these other systems, viewed comparatively, offer studies

---

1 Harvard Law Review, vol. X, pp. 321, 389, vol. XI, p. 18 (1897).
2 "Problems of Law, Its Past, Present and Future" (University of Virginia Lectures, New York, Scribner, 1920).

of *specific institutions* or ideas; e. g. of marriage, inheritance, procedure, and so on.

(1) Now, the tracing of the evolution of specific rules and institutions is of course the ultimate aim, in comparative nomogenetics. But this objective needs, for its completion, an auxiliary study of the systems as such, taking each as a whole. Since the individual rules and institutions are bound and related together, as the gross product of the social and political life of a particular race or people, their evolution cannot be fully understood without first conceiving the whole system, in its political environment and its chronology. E. g. a biologist might make a comparative study of the liver of an African, a Chinese, a Russian, and an Italian; but he could not expect to reach safe conclusions on the liver as a human organ unless he had already studied the complete body in the environment of each of these races, as a composite entity of several other organs in a special origin and environment.

Let us call this mode of treatment the Corporeal method in comparative law. Professor Hozumi, the eminent Japanese jurist, called it the Genealogical method, i. e. "a method which takes for the unit of comparison a certain group of laws having a common lineage or descent".[3] Whether the analogy of a physical body,

---

3 *N. Hozumi*, "The New Japanese Civil Code as Material for the Study of Comparative Jurisprudence", p. 33 (Tokyo, Maruzen, 2d ed. 1912).

rather than of a social family, is the closer, is open to argument. But the term here chosen is Corporeal.

The analogy of language is perhaps the nearest. Speech, like law, is a human and social behavior-product. As the dialects are numbered by thousands, the languages by hundreds, but the families of language by scores only; so the congeries of local customs are numerable by thousands, the groups of national or tribal law by the hundred, but the systems of law by not more than a score. Language-families originate territorially in a dominant race-stock; so do law-systems. Languages may be transferred from the native race-stock to alien race-stocks; so may legal systems. And the study of languages has been vitally assisted by the discovery and historical analysis of language-families. The study of etymological elements, i. e. of particular word-roots and of parts of speech, by taking (as it were) a cross-section of languages in comparison, is one thing, and corresponds to the study of a particular institution, such as contract or mortgage, in different legal systems. But the study of the growth and transformation of a language-family, as a whole, and as the common possession of various peoples having a territory and a history, is a different thing,—the Indo-European family, for example, in Asia and Europe, the Semitic family in Asia and Africa, and the Edo family in

Africa. This corresponds to the study of a legal system, as a corporeal entity, having an external history in time and place, apart from its specific internal institutions. It is this corporeal method in comparative nomogenetics to which we here call attention.

(2) Now, this study of each legal system as a whole was not feasible until very modern times. Nor would it be attractive, in the highest degree, as a basis for broad and safe generalizations, unless we believed that we had before us *virtually all the actual systems*.

The present writer believes that such is now the case. There are, or have been, no more than sixteen or so legal systems in the world. They are these: Egyptian, Mesopotamian, Hebrew, Chinese, Hindu, Greek, Roman, Maritime, Japanese, Mohammedan, Keltic, Germanic, Slavic, Ecclesiastical, Romanesque, Anglican.[1]

---

1 The *Inca* system of law in Peru has not been here considered, for three reasons: (1) the Incas had no system of writing for records (only knotted strings), and hence their law left no records of its own; (2) our knowledge of it comes through the chronicles of their Spanish conquerors, not fully dependable for this purpose; (3) the extant accounts are too scanty for reconstructing the system.

As to *Mexican* (Aztec) literature, it is possible that the future may reveal some materials of a legal system; see *John Hobert Cornyn*, "The Lost Literature of the Aztecs" (Bulletin of the Pan-American Union, LXII, 382, April, 1928).

The *Hungarian* law does not present a new type of system. Though the Hungarian race-stock is Altaic or Turanian, and hence distinct from its neighboring Slavic and Germanic stocks, yet it had not reduced to writing nor developed a legal system in the primitive stage of its arrival in Europe; and its germs were early cultivated in a Romanesque culture (e. g. its legal annals were preserved in Latin from A. D. 1200 for some six centuries); so that it never developed a system of its own.

Whether the *Ethiopian* stock had originally a civilization of its own does not yet appear to be settled. But it very early fell under the influence of the Christianized Roman law-books of Byzantium, and its legal system (such as it is) belongs under the Romanesque type.

The *Hittite* law, so far as the deciphered records yet show, can not be regarded as distinct from the Mesopotamian system.

Of course, every human race and community has had its particular customs of some sort. But just as the biologists draw the great line between invertebrates and vertebrates, and again between animals and humans, so the legal scientist must recognize and set apart the higher forms of socio-legal phenomena, viz. those which represent a body of rules consciously connected and developed as a whole. A legal system is a body of rules having a life of its own, as a part of some political system. Such legal systems react upon themselves, and tend by logic to develop individual details—just as the specific organs of the vertebrate mammal plantigrade homo are modified in details by the subjective process of cerebration, independently of environment. Hence they form a class by themselves for the legal scientist.

(3) Moreover, taking this corporeal life of the whole legal system, we find that it presents some problems of evolution of its own, irrespective of the evolution of particular legal institutions within it. The legal systems are usually found associated, in their beginnings, with a certain race or community having political life. In the course of that life, whole legal systems are seen to disappear or to survive, while the racial, or social, or political life goes on or does not go on. And so, certain questions

peculiar to the evolution of systems force themselves on us. Here are four, at least, for example:

(i) Whether a legal system is a mere occasional by-product of racial social-political life, or is rather an essential *function*?

(ii) Whether occasional or essential, does it come into being by *imitation* of another people (the theory of Tarde, the eminent sociologist) or by inherent psychological necessity (the theory of Del Vecchio, the eminent philosopher)?

(iii) If an essential function, whether a legal system is, in its location, *generic* to all organized humanity, or is only sub-human, i. e. found in certain *species* that are racial or national?

(iv) If racial or national, then, when the race or nation *disappears*, does the legal system disappear? Or, if not (sometimes or often), what is the place and process of its survival; and what the explanation of the anomaly?

(4) To illustrate the possibilities of these questions, as forced upon us by the comparative study of all the systems as wholes, let the following facts be considered, with these tentative generalizations:

Of the world's sixteen systems (as diagnosed by the present writer): (a) Six have disappeared completely (*as*

legal systems), viz. Egyptian, Mesopotamian, Greek, Hebrew, Keltic, Canon; (b) Five survive as hybrids, viz.
Roman, Germanic, Slavic, Maritime, Japanese; (c) Three
survive more or less unmixed, viz. Chinese, Hindu, Mohammedan; (d) Two are new-created as hybrids, viz.
Romanesque, Anglican.

Now it will be noted, of the six that have disappeared,
that their governments or nations also have disappeared,
but that their native race-stocks have not all disappeared,
e. g. Egyptians and Hebrews. "A legal system, then, may
die, without the *race-stock* dying"; is this a sound generalization?

Again: Of the five that survive as hybrids, they are in
two instances no longer associated with race-stocks
(Roman, Maritime). "A legal system, then, may partly
survive, irrespective of the *race-stock*"; is this a sound
generalization?

Again: Of the three that survive unmixed, the race-
stock survives in all, but in two instances (Hindu, Mohammedan) not the government. "A legal system, then,
may survive without the *political system* surviving";
is this a sound generalization?

Again, if we examine the six systems that have disappeared and the three that have survived unmixed, we
find that in three of the first six (Egyptian, Mesopotamian,

Keltic) the *professional class* that administered the law disappeared at the same time; that in the two where the professional class has not disappeared (Hebrew, Canon) the system itself survives but not as law; and that in the sixth (Greek) there never was (in strictness) any professional class. And we find that of the three that survive unmixed, the professional class survived in all (Chinese, Hindu, Mohammedan) in spite of political changes. Moreover, in the two newly created (Romanesque, Anglican), a professional class was the instrument of their creation.

(5) This leads to a generalization (which has become a favorite hypothesis of the present writer's): The principal feature that controls the creation or the survival of a legal system is the rise and persistence of a body of technical legal ideas; and this body of legal ideas is itself the result of the existence of a professional class of legal thinkers or practitioners, who created and preserved the body of ideas independently of the identity of the political system and independently of the purity of the race-stock. In short, *the rise and perpetuation of a legal system is dependent on the development and survival of a highly trained professional class.*

The foregoing generalizations are, of course, merely hypotheses thrown out as worthy of inquiry. But they serve to illustrate the scientific importance of studying each of the several legal systems in its corporeal whole, as a preliminary to the study of the evolution of specific legal ideas or institutions.

The present work, it is hoped, may help to interest many students in this point of view, and thus to place on a broader basis the science of Comparative Legal History.

Appendix

Appendix

A WORLD-MAP OF PRESENT-DAY
LEGAL SYSTEMS

Since the world's legal systems can be identified in area, and are limited in number, the study of them would be assisted by a map showing the areas of the world's surface covered by the respective systems. Changes at successive periods could and should be shown by a series of period-maps (as is done for the history of national and dynastic boundaries). But here, for a first attempt, will be offered only a map of the present-day period.[1]

For reading the map, some explanations must be made as to: A, Classification of Systems; B, Symbols used; C, Ascription of Systems to particular nations or areas.

A. Classification of Systems

Only *systems* can be separately shown, i. e. the few developed bodies of law, not the innumerable unorganized groups of tribal custom.

But all systems now in existence are more or less *mixed* in origin and history, and the various shades of these mixtures are too numerous to be represented. Hence only the

---

[1] This map owes its origin to a suggestion of Col. Lawrence Martin, chief of the map-division of the Library of Congress, following a conference with M. Pierre LePaulle of the Paris Bar, and others, at the Williams College Institute of Politics, in the summer of 1927.

system representing the *present dominant character* or characters of the law in a given nation or area can be shown.

Nevertheless, some mixtures cannot be ignored. In certain areas, to show a single unmixed system would be misleading, and would be valueless for the purpose of analyzing tendencies. Therefore at least four distinctions in types of mixtures, seem necessary, as well as feasible, to represent on the map. These four types are as follows:

(1) *Pure* Systems; i. e. as in England, France.

(2) *National Blends*, i. e. where a people having a native system has adopted in part an alien system (by recasting its native system in alien categories, or otherwise), thus making a single blended system under native sovereignty; as in Japan.

(3) *Colonial Composites*, i. e. where an alien power, holding a colony or protectorate or mandate, has imposed its own political or public law, but continues to preserve and enforce the native system for private law, in part or in whole; as in Algeria.

(4) *Colonial Duplex Composites*, i. e. where an alien power has done as in (3), but enforces two or more native systems for separate classes of natives; India is the only notable example of this.

Extra-territoriality is not here shown, i. e. where a native sovereignty enforces foreign law for the alien residents as a separate class of persons, either in consular courts or in mixed courts; this form of jurisdiction does not add to the types of systems, though it may affect numbers of the population.

On the above four types, the following further comments must be made:

(1) *Pure Systems.* Of the sixteen systems described in the foregoing chapters, only eight can be recognized surviving as such in today's world, viz. Anglican, Chinese, Germanic, Hindu, Japanese, Mohammedan, Romanesque, Slavic.

Of these eight, only four are now found anywhere as pure systems, viz. Anglican, Hindu, Mohammedan, Romanesque; the remaining ones appear only in blends or composites.

(2) *Blends.* The distinction between a blend and a composite is this: In a blend, various institutions from two systems are fused into a single system, under native sovereignty, *applicable to all persons* in the jurisdiction (except extra-territorial exemptions); but in a composite, the two systems remain separate, each being applicable to a *different group of persons.* Thus there might conceivably

[*1135*]

be a *national* composite (and there is, in fact, in Egypt, and elsewhere, and was in imperial Russia, though for groups of persons too small to be here recognized). But on this map the blends are only national, i. e. under native sovereignty, and the composites are only colonial, i. e. under alien sovereignty.

One particular blend calls for special note, viz. the Russian Soviet Federation. Here the foundation is still more or less the historical Romanized Slavic blend, nominally displaced by the Communist system; but the Communist institutions are formulated in Romanesque categories, and at the present time it seems best to class the system as a blend, not a new independent system.

Blends, of course, differ in the *degree of actual application* of the borrowed system as law. E. g. in Japan and Siam the blend has long been thorough; in China it has made substantial start; in Turkey, it is as yet beginning; in Persia it is in embryo. No attempt to show such differences is made on this map.

Blends also differ in the various *parts chosen* from the two systems for blending. E. g. in Scotland and in the South African Republic the elements taken from the Romanesque system would be very different from the Romanesque elements taken by Japan, by China, by

Persia, by Siam. No attempt to show such differences is made on this map.

Blends are of course open to difference of opinion in respect to the *quality* of a blended element that entitles it to recognition for particular nations. For example, Scotland and the South African Republic are commonly classed under the Romanesque system; yet the Anglican element is too large to be ignored; and therefore both those countries are shown on the map as blends. The Scandinavian countries are also commonly classed as Romanesque; yet the Germanic system (obsolete everywhere in its pure form) is there so largely preserved that it cannot justly be ignored, and all of those countries are therefore shown as blends. For these and other countries, the map has chosen solutions which are no doubt open to difference of opinion.

(3) (4) *Composites*. In a composite system, the *number of native* systems (i. e. of "personal" law) that might be actually enforced by an alien sovereignty is of course theoretically large. In some countries, no doubt, it is at least plural. But only the *one* major native system is recognized on this map; i. e. the one in force among the large mass of the population. The only composite country for which two native systems are shown on the map is

India, where Hindu law and Mohammedan law must both be recognized.

Where no organized system is found, but only *local tribal customs,* this infinitely variegated type is represented on the map by a single symbol. It always appears as a composite, of course, because the whole terrestrial surface is now nominally under the sovereignty of one or another national power, and thus the areas in which local tribal custom still obtains are usually under one or another alien power, either as colonies, protectorates, or mandates.— Local tribal custom is of course recognized, or actually in force, in many areas of Asia and of Africa too small to be recognized on the map. Some of them, moreover, are in strictness national composites, not colonial composites.

In the lesser known or more recently dominated areas of Africa and Asia, there are many *border-line regions* where the allotment of systems must of course be tentative only. E. g. in Africa, the region of Mohammedan law (as a composite element) shades off gradually into the region of tribal custom. So, too, in northwestern and north central Asia, the areas of tribal custom, as contrasted with the surrounding Chinese, Hindu, Mohammedan, and Soviet systems, leave many doubtful borderlines. The map here attempts to show no more than broad tendencies.

[*1138*]

As to the *kind of law* (public law, etc.) that is imposed by the alien political power in colonial composite systems, this differs, of course, under different powers. Alien taxation-law and police-law are always found; also more or less penal law, and often judiciary organization. Civil procedure is sometimes included (India), sometimes not (Morocco). No attempt is made to represent these variations on the map.

B.   SYMBOLS

For readiest apprehension, different colors should be used to indicate the several systems. But on this black-and-white map the systems can be adequately shown by the use of *letters*, capital and small, alone and in combination. Thus:

A capital letter alone represents a *pure* system. Two capital letters represent a *blend*. A capital letter and a small letter represent a *composite*.

The letters chosen are the initial letters of the names used above for the systems. The several systems are lettered as follows:

Key to Letter Symbols

A—Anglican System	M—Mohammedan System
C—Chinese System	R—Romanesque System
G—Germanic System	S—Slavic System
H—Hindu System	SS—Soviet Slavic System
J—Japanese System	T—Tribal Customary Law

Blends are lettered thus: AR (Anglican-Romanesque), RC (Romanesque-Chinese).

Composites are lettered thus: Am (Anglican-Moham-medan); Rt (Romanesque-Tribal custom).

Countries (nations, colonies, protectorates, etc.) are indicated by numerical figures. The terrestrial surface is divided into four continents (Africa, America, Asia, Europe) and Oceanica. Within each division the several countries, etc., after being arranged alphabetically, are numbered serially, and this number is placed also on the map at the proper location. Countries and possessions not large enough for map-marks, or not important enough for distinction from adjacent areas, have been ignored.

National boundaries have not been marked by the author; the marks would have confused a map of this size. But on the original Goode map-plate the boundaries are marked, as of 1923, by dotted lines, which can be discerned on this map with the aid of a hand-lens.

C. ASCRIPTION OF SYSTEMS TO PARTICULAR REGIONS

There is of course some room for difference of opinion in the ascription of systems to particular regions, even of those systems that have long been well known. For regions not yet fully described in authentic legal chronicles, there is even more room for controversy by those who have special knowledge of particular areas. The following allotment represents the author's opinion (tentative in many instances) formed in the light of available information:

No. on Map	AFRICA Name	System	No. on Map	AMERICA Name	System
1.	Abyssinia	RT	1.	Argentina	R
2.	Algeria	Rm	2.	Bolivia	R
3.	British S. W. Africa	At	3.	Brazil	R
4.	Congo (Belg.)	Rt	4.	Canada	A
5.	Congo (Fr.)	Rt	5.	Canal Zone	AR
6.	Egypt	M	6.	Cent. Am. States	R
7.	Eretria	Rm	7.	Chile	R
8.	Gold Coast	Am	8.	Columbia	R
9.	Liberia	At	9.	Cuba	R
10.	Libia	Rm	10.	Ecuador	R
11.	Madagascar	Rt	11.	Guiana (Br.)	A
12.	Morocco	Rm	12.	Guiana (D.)	R
13.	Nigeria (Br.)	Am	13.	Guiana (Fr.)	R
14.	Nigeria, etc. (Fr.)	Rm	14.	Honduras (Br.)	A
15.	Port. E. Afr	Rt	15.	Louisiana	AR
16.	Port. W. Afr	Rt	16.	Mexico	R
17.	Rhodesia, Bechuana-land, etc.	At	17.	Paraguay	R
18.	Sierra Leone	Am	18.	Peru	R
19.	Somali (Br.)	Am	19.	Porto Rico	AR
20.	Somali (Ital.)	Rm	20.	Quebec	AR
21.	So. Afr. Rep.	AR	21.	Uruguay	R
22.	Sudan	Am	22.	U. S. America	A
23.	Tanganyika	Atm	23.	Venezuela	R
24.	Tripoli	Rm	24.	West Ind. Islands (Br.)	A
25.	Tunisia	Rm	25.	West Ind. Islands (Fr.)	R
26.	Uganda and Kenya	Am			

No. on Map	ASIA Name	System	No. on Map	EUROPE Name	System
1.	Afghanistan	M	1.	Albania	RS
2.	Annam	Rc	2.	Austria	R
3.	Arabia (remainder)	M	3.	Belgium	R
4.	Beluchistan	Am	4.	Bulgaria	RS
5.	Bokhara	M	5.	Czechoslovakia	RS
6.	Burma	Ah	6.	Denmark	RG
7.	Cambodia	Rh	7.	England & Wales	A
8.	China	RC	8.	Esthonia	RG
9.	East Ind. Isl. (Br.)	Am	9.	Finland	RG
10.	East Ind. Isl. (D.)	Rm	10.	France	R
11.	Hejaz	M	11.	Germany	R
12.	India	Amh	12.	Greece	R
13.	Irak	M	13.	Greenland	RG
14.	Japan	RJ	14.	Hungary	R
15.	Korea	RJ	15.	Iceland	RG
16.	Manchuria	RC	16.	Ireland	A
17.1	Mongolia (Inner)	RCh	17.	Italy	R
17.2	Mongolia (Outer)	RSSh	18.	Latvia	RG
18.	Palestine	Am	19.	Lithuania	RS
19.	Persia	RM	20.	Netherlands	R
20.	Phil. Isl	AR	21.	Norway	RG
21.	Siam	RH	22.	Poland	RS
22.	Siberia	RSS	23.	Portugal	R
23.	Syria	Rm	24.	Rumania	RS
24.	Tibet	H	25.	Russia	RSS
25.	Tonkin	Rc	26.	Scotland	AR
26.1	Turkestan (Russian)	M	27.	Spain	R
26.2	Turkestan (Chinese)	RCm	28.	Sweden	RG
27.	Turkish Rep.	RM	29.	Switzerland	R
			30.	Yugoslavia	RS

OCEANICA

No. on Map	Name	System
1.	Australia............A	
2.	Hawaiian Isl.........A	

No. on Map	Name	System
3.	{ Melanesia { Micronesia	...... { At { Rt
4.	New Zealand.........A	

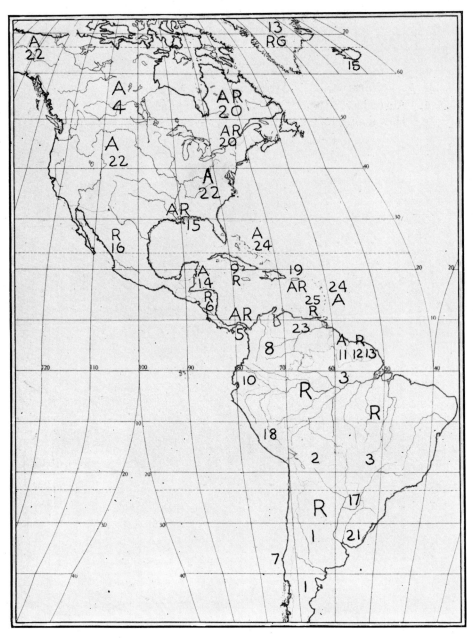

SHEET 1: WORLD-MAP OF PRESENT-DAY LEGAL SYSTEMS
Made on J. Paul Goode's Outline Homolosine Map 101 HC
(Key on p. 1139. Greenland and Iceland are keyed to Europe)

[1144]

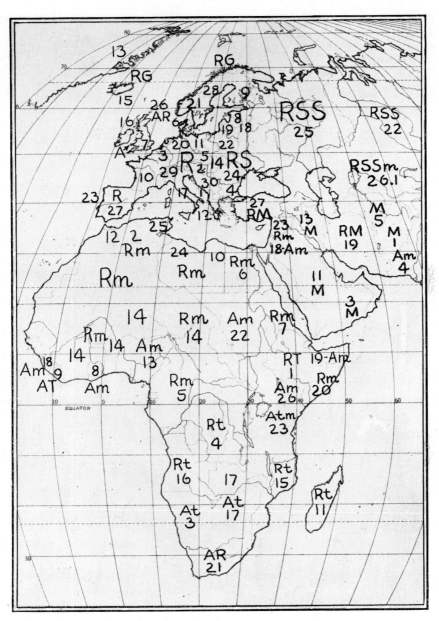

SHEET 2: WORLD-MAP OF PRESENT-DAY LEGAL SYSTEMS
(Key on p. 1139)

[1145]

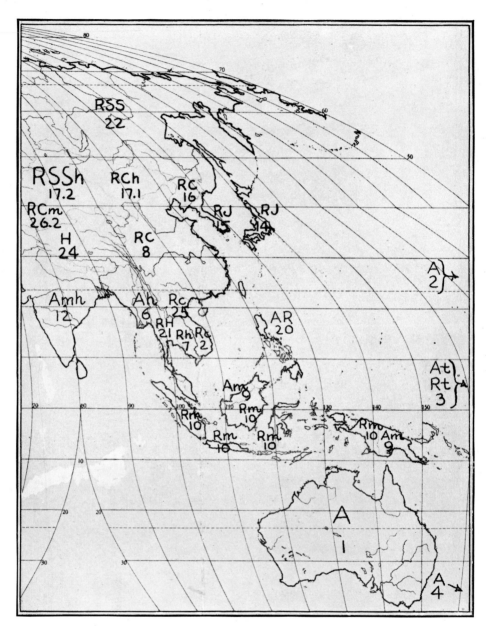

SHEET 3: WORLD-MAP OF PRESENT-DAY LEGAL SYSTEMS
(Key on p. 1139. Pacific Islands are indicated at the right)

[1146]

LIST OF ILLUSTRATIONS

[References are to pages]

[*1147*]

III. THE HEBREW LEGAL SYSTEM

IV. THE CHINESE LEGAL SYSTEM

VII.   THE ROMAN LEGAL SYSTEM

VIII. THE JAPANESE LEGAL SYSTEM

IX. The Mohammedan Legal System

X. The Keltic Legal System

XI. THE SLAVIC LEGAL SYSTEM

XII. The Germanic Legal System

XIII. THE MARITIME LEGAL SYSTEM

[*1158*]

Index

Index

A

Index

Index

Index

Index

Index

Index

Index

Index

Index

Index

Index

Index

Index

Index

Index

[1189]

Index

Index

Index

Index

Index

Index

Index

Index

Index

(PRINTED IN U. S. A.)